11.50

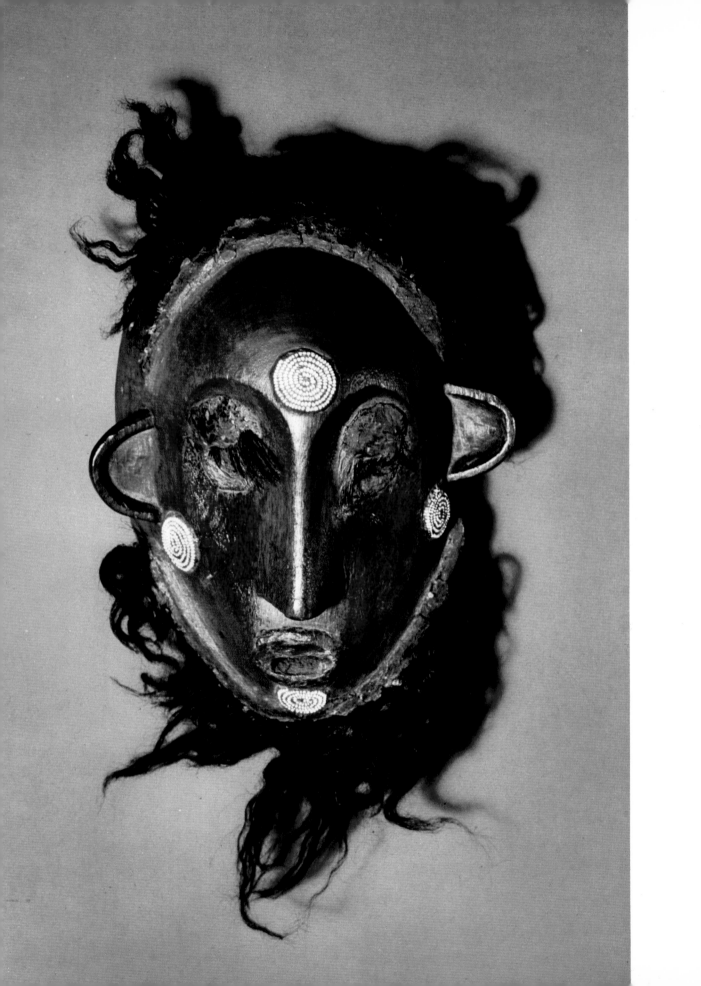

The Art of Africa

# MASKS AND FIGURES

## from Eastern and Southern Africa

Ladislav Holý

Photographed by
Dominique Darbois

PAUL HAMLYN · LONDON

Text by Ladislav Holý, edited by Margret Carey
from the translation by Till Gottheiner
Notes on the Plates by Margret Carey
Photographs by Dominique Darbois and Oster, Musée de l'Homme, Paris
Graphic design by Karel Pánek
Designed and produced by Artia for
Paul Hamlyn Ltd
Drury House, Russell Street, London, W. C. 2
© 1967 by Artia, Prague
Printed in Czechoslovakia by Polygrafia, Prague
S 2199

# LIST OF CONTENTS

East and South Africa is sometimes considered 'a region without art', an area in which art was suppressed by the influence of Hamite culture and that of the nomadic cattle-grazing tribes, who lacked the settled life needed to develop art. Exceptions are found in the wooden sculptures and masks of certain Mozambique tribes (the Makonde, Yao, Mawia), which show the influence of the 'West African style' that penetrated East Africa as far as the shores of the Indian Ocean. Apart from a few isolated examples of art among certain other East African tribes, the entire vast territory of East and South Africa has been by-passed by all writers on African art. The one exception to this rule is Eckart von Sydow (1954), who was the first to draw attention to the fact that there was art to be found in the vast territories of East and South Africa. Mapping the few known facts on East African sculpture reveals clearly that in East Africa there are only a very few tribes where no forms of art have yet been discovered. It is quite certain, moreover, that the brief survey of art in East and South Africa given in this book is far from complete. Further examples of that art may be seen in many other museums in Europe and particularly in Africa, to whose collections we, unfortunately, did not have access. Other facts are likely to be included in specialist papers beyond our reach.

This book does not even set out to render a comprehensive account, but simply to show that art exists in that part of the world and that East and South African sculpture, low though its average level is in comparison with West African work, grew out of very similar roots of thought. Should this book stimulate deeper interest in the art of East and South Africa, it will have fully achieved its aim.

**L**ike all Islamic countries the northern Sudan with its predominantly Arab or Arab-influenced population is a region of comparatively highly developed arts and crafts, such as richly ornamented hampers and flat coil-sewn wicker baskets made from coloured grass, leather articles and ceramics. Free-standing sculpture hardly exists in the northern Sudan, neither among the Arab population, where this may be due to the Islamic prohibition of depicting the human form, nor among the Negro tribes living in the area, many of which resisted Islamic influence.

The only mention of the existence of sculpture in the northern Sudan is to be found in Frobenius' book — where he writes about carved wooden statuettes of men in the men's houses of Nuba, to which the elders of the families sacrificed food and drink at harvest time (Frobenius, 1923, Vol. III, p. 116). Some museum collections possess dolls from the northern Sudan (plates 1–4). Their heads are modelled of camel dung or clay, and covered with fibre hair. The body, wrapped in a garment, is always made of wood. Numerous ornaments of beads, necklaces and leg-rings are imitations of the local women's manner of dress.

**I**n the territory of the southern Sudan there exist in a number of tribes wooden and clay sculptures and masks. Among these tribes are the Ingassana, a small agricultural and cattle-rearing people (12,000 persons), living in the most southerly Blue Nile province of the Sudan, near the Ethiopian border. The British Museum collections include the clumsily carved figure (plate 5), whose appearance is akin to the style of the southern Sudanese Bari and Dinka tribes. Fabrics, beads and hair have been used to make the carving more realistic.

The Nilotic agricultural and cattle-rearing tribes of the Shilluk living on the White Nile around Malakal, the capital of the Upper Nile province of the Sudan, make masks out of gourds, on to which cattle dung is stuck (plate 6; others illustrated by Seligman, 1924). Such masks are to be found in museums in Berlin, Frankfurt, Hamburg and Leipzig ( von Sydow, Pl. 95). The shape and modelling of the masks is governed by the material used. They are circular, slightly elongated, with circular holes for eyes and mouth. The nose is modelled in a straight protruding line. Fish-bones, indicating teeth, are inserted into the mouth aperture. These dancing masks represent leopards, or other animals such as giraffes or lions (Hofmayr, p. 495).

Shilluk sculpture proper takes the form of clay figurines of bulls. They are depicted in Baumann's book (p. 230, Pl. 234), who describes them as cattle fertility symbols *(deang)*. Westermann and Hofmayr mention wooden statues of the god Nyikang, placed in some sanctuaries to this god. They are lifesize, made as a likeness of the ruler, who to the Shilluk is the embodiment of the god Nyikang; they are only roughly carved (Westermann, p. 8; Hofmayr, p. 205). Unfortunately, we have been unable to find an illustration.

In the British Museum Shilluk art is represented in a clay figurine of a hyena (plate 7). The modelling of the little figure shows understanding of the animal's characteristic features. The effect of the sculpture is intensified by contrasting dark red and white colours; we are probably dealing with a modern work.

The existence of wood carving is equally problematic in the case of the Dinka, a large tribe living in the vast expanses of the Upper Nile and Bahr el Ghazal provinces in the southern Sudan. Schweinfurth and Cummins report that the Dinka make only small clay or pottery figurines representing goats, cattle, elephants and other animals. They are probably used as toys and may well be made by the children themselves (Schweinfurth, 1874, vol. I, p. 178; Cummings, p. 160).

In the Museum für Völkerkunde in Berlin Dinka tribal art is represented by a wooden sculpture of a standing man (plate 8). It is a typical pole sculpture. The tall slim body is carved in a primitive manner out of a narrow piece of wood, and the arms hanging alongside the body are carved out of the same piece. The small round head is greatly simplified: circular apertures instead of eyes and ears and rectangular projections with irregular notches indicating lips and teeth; the nose is shown by a triangle. Since Schweinfurth said that the Dinka had no wooden sculpture, the attribution of this figure may be incorrect. Its style resembles the wooden statues of the Bari.

Equally open to discussion is the existence of wood-carving among the Djour group of tribes who depend on cultivation and cattle-keeping. About 20,000 of them live today in scattered groups in the provinces of Bahr el Ghazal, Equatoria and Upper Nile in the southern Sudan. The British Museum possesses two wooden pipes carved to resemble a cylindrical human body with stiff arms, which are completely or partially attached to the block forming the body. The head and legs of the two figures show signs of very simple modelling (plates 9, 10). Although there can be no doubt of the related style of the two figures they differ clearly in execution. The pipes are labelled 'Djour or Gooboo Sobat Tribes, Sudan' and 'Djour or Gooboo near Equator, Central Africa, Sobat Tribes'. In view of the location near the Sobat river it is rather doubtful whether we are really dealing with Djour work. Further doubt as to whether we are, in fact, dealing with sculptures of a Nilotic tribe is roused by the marked tattooing on one of the figures, which does not appear among known Nilotic sculpture. They are closer to female sculptures from the Lake Victoria region, published by Himmelheber (Himmelheber, Pl. 336).

We have proof of wooden sculpture among the Bari, a tribe of about 35,000 people living in the area along both banks of the Nile in the southern Sudanese province of Equatoria. Originally the Bari were a pastoral tribe. In the course of Arab attacks during the nineteenth century most of them were deprived of their cattle and today they are largely dependent on agriculture.

European collections possess at least 45 sculptures from the Bari, to be seen in Berlin, Geneva, Liverpool, London, Oxford, Vienna, Venice (Whitehead, pp. 265 f.), Paris (Paulme, p. 113), Stuttgart and Leningrad. All or most of the exhibits were probably collected in the nineteenth century, some of them in its first half. The figures attributed to the Bari, though all pole sculptures, show certain variations, which might well cause doubts as to their common origin. The collections in the Vienna Museum are relatively unified (plate 11). Their economical, simplified form is stressed by the predominantly vertical lines: the long trunk on long pillar-like legs, arms hanging down the side of the body, the stylized conception of the head, which is elongated and pointed at the crown. Sculptures in the Musée de l'Homme (plates 14, 15) and the Linden-Museum in Stuttgart (plate 13) are of a similar type. By contrast, the figure in Berlin (plate 12) shows a greater interest in anatomy, with a less rigid pose and a feeling for plastic form. The sculpture in the Venice Museum (Seligman, 1928, Pl. XLIII) differs entirely from the pole style of Bari sculpture. Seligman says that the Bari, living on the eastern banks of the Nile, had no idea of the existence of such wooden statues and for that reason he attributed them to the Bari-speaking tribes on the western banks, where they might be related to the sculpture of the Zande and Bongo. (Seligman, 1925, p. 25; Seligman, 1928, p. 411). Junker and Mounteney-Jephson considered that these sculptures portrayed ancestors (Junker, pp. 253, 496; Mounteney-Jephson, pp. 140–1). This view was adopted by later investigators, who thought them imitations of Bongo sculpture (for example Seligman, 1932, p. 474). Paulme is of the opinion that the smaller size of the Bari sculpture as compared with that of the Bongo is due to the Bari custom of keeping their statuettes inside their huts (Paulme, p. 113). On the whole, little is known of the function of Bari sculpture. Seligman quotes Stigand as saying that the statuettes representing dead ancestors (parents) used to be suspended in the huts (Seligman, 1928, p. 411), while Whitehead and Thomas write that they were kept inside the huts where libations were offered to them (Whitehead, p. 265).

Akin to the Bari sculptures are those of the Bongo, a small agricultural tribe living on the savannah along the border of the Bahr el Ghazal and Equatoria provinces of the southern Sudan. The wooden sculptures of the Bongo depict the dead. The larger, almost lifesize statues (1.30 metres/4½ feet tall) serve as tomb figures. Whole rows of such figures stand on the graves of well-known persons with a statue depicting the deceased himself at the front. In execution they are the simplest form of pole figure. They are made out of a roughly worked pole; only the head and sexual symbols are worked in greater detail.

Similar human figures used to stand in the villages, where they represented ornamental elements in the stockade or served as carved gate posts. Sculptures of famous ancestors (njere) were likewise placed in their huts (Schweinfurth, 1872, p. 88; 1874, p. 150; 1875, Pl. 8, figs. 5–8 and caption; Seligman, 1917, p. 97; von Sydow, Pl. 134).

Figures representing brave hunters and warriors stood along both sides of the way leading to the village (von Sydow, p. 96). One of these statuettes, belonging to the British Museum, shows a stiff, pole-like figure lacking all modelling. The arms alongside the body and pillar-shaped legs without any signs of modelling stress the vertical pole character. The head of the figure is more rounded, the face concave, and eyes, nose and mouth are given only in rudimentary form.

The Bongo also made sculptures of murdered men which played a role in the trial designed to discover the killer: the sculpture of the killed person was placed in the centre of the group gathered in a circle so that the murderer should betray himself by his restlessness at the sight of the sculpture.

Not only dead men but even dead women were depicted. Their statuettes, called moiago-kamara, were carved out of hard wood and were about 65–100 centimetres (25–40 inches) high. Rows of beads were hung round their necks and the widowers kept them in their huts.

All sculptures of the deceased were made by the Bongo with a clear effort to achieve as close a likeness as possible. To increase the resemblance the statuettes were adorned with beads and bracelets belonging to the deceased and even hair was stuck to the relevant places (Schweinfurth, 1872, p. 88).

Cudgels and wooden sticks had handles carved roughly in the shape of human heads (H. Baumann, p. 247). Among other Bongo objects Schweinfurth cites small clay pipes in the shape of a human head (Schweinfurth, 1874, p. 154). Even string instruments had ornamental carved heads, as among the Zande (von Sydow, p. 96).

Similar in style to Bongo wood-carvings are the portraits of the dead among the neighbouring Mittu and Sofi tribes. They are likewise decorated with rows of beads or other ornaments (Schweinfurth, 1875, pl. 8).

The art of the Bongo and Mittu forms a transition to the tribes inhabiting the central Sudan, where similar tomb sculptures can be found among the Sara, west of the Shari river. (H. Baumann, pp. 251–2).

## SOUTH-WESTERN ETHIOPIA

Sculpture in south-western Ethiopia takes the form of tomb sculpture. The stones, more than 2 metres (6½ feet) high, in the south-west territory of the Arusi (Galla) usually bear engraved ornaments, filled in with red clay or soot mixed with grease; some depict human figures in rough relief, showing the deceased with cartridge belts around the body and sword in hand. These tombstones are of modern origin, probably inspired by the figures on Islamic tombs, or pictures and photographs which the Arusi might have seen among the Amhara and Europeans. The graves of the Arusi who have been superficially converted to Islam, are, in contrast to the pagan graves, rich in representational ornaments. As among the pagan Arusi there stand around the grave six or eight ornamental stelae, while the centre of the grave takes the form of a step-pyramid with a rough stone statue of a human figure at the top. The graves are usually decorated with sculptured or relief figures carved into the side edges of the tombstones. The head, arms and trunk of the figures are angular. Facial features are indicated simply by apertures. There are no such statues to be found on the tombs of the orthodox Somali or Arabs, whom the Islamic Arusi consider semi-pagans. It remains an open question why Islam with its hatred for pictures and particularly the representational arts became the bearer of that art in Ethiopia while it remained quite unknown among the other Galla (Haberland, 1963a, pp. 495–500; Pl. 32, fig. 6, Pl. 78, fig. 3, Pl. 79, figs. 3, 5; Haberland, 1963b, pp. 108–9, Pl. 2, fig. 3, Pl. 3, figs. 1, 3).

Wooden tombstones or statues depicting the deceased are known among the Konso, Gato and Ometo, Cushite tribes that cultivate the soil and keep cattle in the neighbourhood of the pastoral Galla. The style of their tombstones is in many ways similar to that of the Bongo. The roughly carved wooden pole, without indication of arms or legs, has the head carved with angular features. The faces of individual sculptures show little differentiation, while their unity of style is striking. The face with expressive tubular eyes and sharply carved straight nose is surrounded by a beard and long hair. On the head is a helmet-like cap, sometimes with a phallic symbol. The Konso figures are usually painted red, their eyes are filled in with ostrich eggshell, and the caps on their heads vary in shape.

Among the Gato these rough wooden sculptures (plates 16, 17) are placed in enclosed graveyards lying right in the centre of the village (von Sydow, Pl. 135A). On each grave, whether of men or women, stands one or more of those wooden figures. The social status of the deceased, his wealth or number of wives are symbolized in the necklaces and bracelets of the grave figures. Apart from wooden figures, stone statues have been found on the territory of the Gato, though the Gato today know nothing of their origin. They are smaller-sized pumice stone stelae with roughly worked faces (Jensen, p. 455) or simple phallic columns in granite or basalt (Jensen, p. 448).

Among the Konso the statues of the dead, made only for brave and outstanding men, are not placed on the graves lying outside the villages but at the entrance to the village itself. They stand surrounded by smaller figures of monkeys resembling human beings, constructions of branches representing the body of the animals, symbols of the deceased's hunts and wooden spears made to resemble the real ones the dead man captured. Some such groups of sculptures are very large; Jensen accounts for 21 statues (Jensen, Pl. 141; von Sydow, Pl. 135B). Sometimes the wooden statues have been replaced by groups of stones of which the largest with the face marked in white paint, represents the deceased (Jensen).

The rough pole statues on the graves of the Konso must have their origin in different ideas, e. g. those of the cannibalistic mythical monster *bulgu*, commonly known among the Galla tribes. Each tribe has its own ideas as to its appearance, but all agree on it being ghastly. The Konso themselves think that the *bulgu* has a face at each side of the head. One Konso, who was of the opinion that he saw such a monster in his youth, was so influenced by the image that on his tomb he had it represented in sculpture together with figures of animals and people killed by the monster (Haberland, 1963a, pp. 574–5 Pl. 28, fig. 4). The *bulgu* statue resembles others of their pole statues and their idea of the monster *bulgu*: a roughly worked pole finished with a carved head with a double face. By contrast to other tombstone sculptures of the Konso, it does not have a helmet-shaped cap on its head and hair and beard are absent.

Wooden sculpture—in the form of gravestones—exists also further north, among the Cushite Ometo (Frobenius, 1923, Pl. 173).

Wooden pole sculptures in the ethnological collection at Zurich, attributed by Leuzinger to the Borana (Leuzinger, p. 207, Pl. 62), and which in her view depict brave men and outstanding warriors, should be ascribed to the Konso, with whom the Borana had close contacts (Haberland, 1963a, pp. 148–50). The only sculptures of the Borana are children's toys of clay and dung, representing little figures of sheep and cattle (Haberland, 1963a, Pl. 28, figs. 4, 5, 6).

The sculptures of a number of tribes living in the central part of East Africa, in the territory of Tanzania and the adjoining areas of southern Uganda and southern Kenya, are known from museum exhibits and literature. There is great variety in their art which includes figures carved in wood, masks, small clay models and even iron statuettes. Certain groups can be discerned among them with a given measure of unity in style. The division of artistic areas is more or less arbitrary for that part of the world. Attention will later be drawn to the inter-relations in style among East African tribes.

The first group of tribes where works of art can be found are those living in the interlacustrine area and tribes occupying the land along the eastern shores of Lake Tanganyika; the second group is formed by tribes in Central Tanzania; the third encompasses the Bantu tribes of the north-east; the fourth group is formed by tribes living along the shores of the Indian Ocean, and the last one by those in southern Tanzania.

Among the tribes living in the area bordered to the east by Lake Victoria, and to the west by the string of Central African lakes—Albert, Edward, Kivu and Tanganyika—works of art are known only among the Ziba and Karagwe occupying the territory along the southern end of the western shores of Lake Victoria. The Uganda Museum has on exhibition three wooden masks from the territory of the Busoga, to the north of Lake Victoria (Trowell, p. 2) while the British Museum possesses a sculpture depicting one of the chiefs of the Ganda, whose style, according to Fagg, is strikingly reminiscent of Kerewe sculptures (Fagg, p. 39).

The art of the Ziba takes the form of masks (plates 18–20). They are of oval shape, with an almost straight nose projecting out of the flat mask, flanked by circular apertures for eyes. Human teeth are set in the elongated mouth opening, and painted lines run down the face, tracing even the line of the nose and eyes. The beards are made of monkey fur. In overall appearance, both in shape and flat modelling, these masks recall the Shilluk leopard masks made of gourd. Unfortunately, we possess little detailed information about their exact function. Stuhlmann, who published masks analogous to those depicted in this book, says that they are masks of a court jester (Rehse, p. 64).

Iron animal figures are known from the neighbouring tribe of the Karagwe (plates 21–3). Their main features are simple, of elegant shape, with a true likeness to the depicted object. Such a high evel of art was rarely achieved in Africa. All the known iron figures come from the palace of Rumanika, the ruler of the Karagwe, where Stanley discovered them in 1876. The treasure of metal figures belonging to chief Rumanika contained, apart from those iron figurines of animals, spear points with intertwined ornamental bars, the exact purpose of which is not quite clear; they might have served as fan-holders; there were copper anchors and a figure of a bird made of copper foil (plate 24), (Stuhlmann, pp. 76–7). But in comparison with the iron animal figures its appearance is slightly stilted.

A primitive figure of a bird is the only sculpture known from Urundi (plate 25). The absence of sculpture in Urundi and neighbouring Ruanda was confirmed by Meyer, who says that carved wooden figures are to be found only among the Rundi living on the shore of Lake Tanganyika, an art introduced from the Congo (Meyer, pp. 81, 137). Some authors believe that wooden masks exist both in Ruanda and Urundi (Trowell, p. 2).

The sculpture of the neighbouring Ha tribe, of whom about 180,000 live on the territory north-east of Lake Tanganyika, is rather limited. In the Museum in Berlin they are represented by a wooden sculpture (plate 26) carved simply, with an expressionless face, wrapped in coloured cotton garments.

Expressive sculpture is found only among the Jiji, living on the eastern shores of northern Lake Tanganyika (plates 27, 28). They are sometimes considered an ethnic group belonging to the Ha tribe. Their wooden figures show an elongated cylindrical trunk and neck with short bent legs. The curves of arms and legs and the stylized scarification on face and torso lend interest to the carvings. Apart from wooden figurines the Jiji, like the Fipa, make stools in the shape of human beings (von Sydow, p. 102).

The Vinza, who are the Jiji's neighbours along the eastern shores of Lake Tanganyika, seem to make only clay figures, used for magic and religious cults (Cory, 1956, p. 172).

The Bende, living further south, who occupy the central region along the eastern shores of Lake Tanganyika, have very characteristic sculpture. As in the case of the Jiji, their figures stress the cylindrical shape of body and trunk, which are elongated, with a lowered centre of gravity, the stiffness of the figure being relieved by bent arms; hair surrounds the face.

The figure shown here (plate 29) is one of three Bende sculptures in the Berlin Museum. It was found in an abandoned hut in 1901. The collector stated that these figures would be obtained from Urua at the death of the chief, when a slave was sacrificed to them. Since they come from Urua they cannot have been made by the Bende tribe. Urua was the name given to the territory lying west of the southern end of Lake Tanganyika (the 'Kasong Empire') inhabited by the Luba tribes. The foreign provenance of sculpture found on Bende territory would explain certain stylistic resemblances with Luba sculpture, to which Fagg drew attention (Fagg, pp. 39, 64). Bende contact with the territory to the west of Lake Tanganyika is further indicated by the fact that among the Bende lived many members of the Hololholo tribe who are settled along the western shores of the lake (Murdock, p. 359).

Among the Fipa, living to the east of the southern point of Lake Tanganyika, sculpture is limited, it appears, to some carved wooden headrests and stools (plates 30, 31).

## CENTRAL TANZANIA

Quite an unusual style in wooden figures was devised by the Kerewe, whose 40,000 inhabitants live on the island of Ukerewe near the south-eastern point of Lake Victoria and the adjacent parts of the mainland. Their figures (plate 33) have cylindrical bodies—trunk, legs, arms—and not even the bent legs enliven the movement or manage to overcome the overall stiffness of appearance. Modelling is given in rough outline. The Kerewe figures depict dead ancestors, mainly chiefs, to whom, it seems, no sacrifices were offered (O. Baumann, 1894, pp. 1213 f.; Kollman, p. 97; Kroll, pp. 142–4).

The large Sukuma tribe (about 1,000,000), living on the territory of north-eastern Tanzania to the south of Lake Victoria, is famous for wood and clay sculpture. Like the Kerewe the wooden figures of the Sukuma have cylindrical bodies and limbs with stylization of details (plates 32, 34). This applies similarly to their clay figures (plate 35), which probably served as children's toys and were used during initiation ceremonies to secret societies (Cory, 1956, p. 172). Baumann, who published one of these clay figures, says that the female statue with bead loin cloth was used, attached to a pole, during dances of the spirits (O. Baumann, 1894, p. 236). The Sukuma decorated even their string instruments with carved human figures (H. Baumann, p. 192).

The Nyamwezi tribe, living on cultivation and cattle-breeding, with a population of more than half a million people, is settled over a vast area in Central Tanzania. Art forms include toys (Blohm, vol. II, pl. X, figs. 132–7) of all kinds. The simplest are highly stylized animal figures. Their wooden toys are inspired by daily life and we find among them figures of European soldiers, natives, etc., made more realistic by being wrapped in garments. Their subject-matter shows that they are fairly recent.

Other objects made by the Nyamwezi include poles with figures of ancestors, called *ilanga kumbu-limbuli* or *ilanga bya mizimu*. They have all the typical features of pole figures. The body usually forms part of the pole. At the top they end in relatively small heads with concave faces and stylized features. The men who carried these poles paid respect to the ancestors depicted on them, and as users enjoyed their protection (Blohm, vol. II, Pl. 12, figs. 162–3).

Certain objects of everyday use were given carvings of human figures, for example, pipe-stems (plate 36). By contrast to pole figures these are worked in more detail but show identical stylization and elongated necks.

Free-standing sculpture was much rarer. Blohm published some primitive statuettes representing, in his view, figures of female ancestors (Blohm, vol. II, Pl. XII, fig. 164). Here, too, the stylization of form is, in principle, identical. Bösch mentions a human figure in clay used during initiation ceremonies of the Baswezi secret society, which depicted the god or hero Lyangolmbe, to whom the society was consecrated. The figure had three projections on the head and other elongated ones on the back (Bösch, p. 212). According to Cory the clay models were used during wedding ceremonies, at celebrations of the birth of the first child and even during magic and religious cults (Cory, 1956, p. 172).

In contrast to this rather primitive art of the Nyamwezi stands the carving on the chief's throne (plate 37) as unique in composition and shape. It was taken from the palace of the Sultaness at Buruku in 1898. A human figure in high relief sprawls asymmetrically across the elongated back of the chair. The head and outstretched arms stretch beyond the back of the chair. The straight parts of the body, again cylindrical in shape, are stressed even on this figure. The trunk is elongated in relation to the rest of the figure and the centre of gravity is lowered through the bent legs. This chair is similar to the throne of the chief of the Gogo, living to the east of the Nyamwezi. It now belongs to the museum in Vienna (von Sydow, Pl. 136C).

The style of the two chairs resembles the carving on two horns, probably powder-horns or snuff-bottles, in a private collection, and said to be of Rhodesian or Tanzanian origin (plates 38, 39). One horn is shaped like a stylized woman with a carved head at the mouthpiece and arms in relief. On the other side is a relief of her child almost identical in execution with that on the Nyamwezi chair.

As for the Turu, the eastern neighbours of the Nyamwezi, we have only a mention of clay figures. These figures were used during the boys' initiation ceremonies (Cory, 1956, p. 172).

The Sumbwa, living next to the Nyamwezi to the north-east, have similar customs to the Nyamwezi in using clay figures during ceremonies held on the birth of the first child and during other magic and religious cults (Cory, 1956, p. 172).

Other Central Tanzanian tribes, whose sculpture is represented in museum collections, include the Hehe, living to the south of the Gogo. They produced primitive animal figures. Even with all their rough modelling they caught the typical shape of the depicted animal (plate 41). They also decorated their staffs with carvings of human heads (plate 42). These are globular with incised details, from which only the nose projects. Artistically far more interesting than those clay figures and sticks with carved human heads is a wooden statue in the Hamburg museum (plate 40). It represents a standing figure of a woman with a long cylindrical body spreading at the hips and low bent knees. The circular head on the long neck has a flat nose and wide open eyes. The feeling for detail is far greater in the case of this sculpture than any other work of art known from the area. This is strikingly reminiscent of a large female figure belonging to a private collection and published by Himmelheber (Himmelheber, Pl. 336). The collector says that it came from the eastern shores of Lake Victoria. Its similarity to the Hehe figure applies not only to the overall appearance and proportions of the body, that is, the elongated cylindrical body broadening at the hips, the shortened legs and bent arms placed across the abdomen and the circular head on a cylindrical neck, but also to the modelling of the face, the scarification, etc. Himmelheber sees even certain similarities to the art of the Rotse (Lozi) carvers.

The tribes of the plateau area in Central Tanzania seem to lack any form of art. The only exception, taken with a grain of salt perhaps, might be the mask of the Iraku (Umbulu) tribe, in the Linden-Museum at Stuttgart (plate 43). It is worth mentioning not so much for its artistic value as for its conception, which generally tallies with the style of East African masks met so far. It is difficult to label it as a form of sculpture. The flat leather mask with small coloured beads set in geometrical patterns is broken up only by the square-shaped apertures for eyes and mouth. This mask of primitive execution shows a certain relation to the masks of the Shilluk and Ziba.

## NORTH-EASTERN BANTU

This term is used to label the Bantu tribes living in the mountain areas in north-eastern Tanzania and in southern Kenya—the tribes of the Kikuyu, Kamba, Chaga, Kahe and Pare. Their forms of self-expression are clay figurines.

The Chaga, living on the southern slopes of Mount Kilimanjaro, produce very primitive anthropomorphic clay figures, known as *nungu*. A series of these sculptures belongs to the Néprajzi Museum in Budapest. Vajda distinguishes eight types of such sculptures (Vajda, 1953, pp. 210 ff.). The first (plate 44) has a cylindrical body with the head schematically depicted by horizontal notches along the cylinder of the figure and two rows of projections along the edge of the body. In between at both ends are circular apertures marking the mouth and the vagina. The second type differs from the first only by a different form of stylization of the head, which has the shape of a little pipe sticking out of the figure. The third, similarly reminiscent of the first, has an irregular cylindrical shape and lacks the typical belly groove of the preceding type. The fourth type (plate 46) retains the cylindrical shape and the two rows of projections on the belly, but the head is more carefully depicted with facial features. It even has female genitals. The fifth type of *nungu* clay figure (plate 47) is similar to the preceding but differs in the arrangement of the projections set in several rows. Closely connected is the sixth type with male genitals and the seventh where sexual symbols are not clear. According to Vajda the eighth type includes various sculptures lacking careful marking of the head and face and confused or non-existent genitals (plate 45).

The *nungu* were used as a means of searching out those who had committed some crime. They were endowed with magic power and, as a result, were said to be able to destroy the criminal (for a closer study of the *nungu* see Vajda, 1953).

We lack closer information on the ideas aroused by clay figures or their function among other tribes of the north-eastern Bantu, where the figures are of far higher artistic level than the primitive ones of the Chaga. The Kikuyu, living in the territory between Nairobi and Mount Kenya, used clay figures during dances held at harvest time once every two years (Routledge, 1910, p. 108). The clay figures of the Kikuyu (plate 48) are roughly worked, representing seated male and female figures. The massive block of the roughly cylindrical trunk has crudely modelled projections forming legs and arms with stumpy fingers. On the short neck sits a spherical head with roughly marked ears. There are holes for the eyes and small pieces of grass stem are inserted in the mouth for teeth. Routledge published other examples of Kikuyu clay figures (for example, Routledge 1910, Pls 117 ff.; Routledge, 1906). He reports that in the potting areas even children made their own toy animal figures of unburnt clay. Such clay dolls can be found among the neighbouring Kamba, who live in the territory between Mount Kenya and Kilimanjaro (Lindblom, Pl. 118).

Similar clay modelling is known among the Kahe, who are sometimes taken as belonging to the Chaga group of tribes (plate 49), among the Pare, living in the mountainous region of that name in north-eastern Tanzania, south-east of Kilimanjaro (plate 51) and the Nilotic Arusha, the eastern neighbours of the Chaga, who belong to the group of Masai tribes, but differ from them in their agricultural way of life (plate 50).

The figures of the Kahe, Pare and Arusha are undoubtedly related to the clay sculptures of the Chaga and Kikuyu, both in the material used and the general appearance. But they show much more sensitive modelling, more complex features and facial traits, even if rudimentary in execution. The Kahe sculptures even show an indication of movement. Their arms and legs do not hang stiffly from the body but are bent in natural movement and fairly sensitively modelled. The depicted figurine of the Kahe was used, according to the collector, for religious cults; the Pare sculptures, according to the same source, used to be placed in the yard of the dwelling to drive away thieves and enemies. We are clearly dealing with figures of magical power, a fact confirmed by Germann (Germann, 1911, pp. 67 ff., Pl. 16, figs. 1, 2).

Cory, too, published a number of Pare clay models (Cory, 1956). They are either stylized figures of animals, sometimes in colour, or simply-moulded human figures with cylindrical bodies, arms and legs, spherical heads, and simple facial features. Figural compositions appear relatively frequently, even figures in action. These clay models were used during initiation ceremonies for boys and girls, where they served as aids in teaching young girls and boys the social values of their society.

Among the tribes of the north-eastern Bantu sculptures in wood are far less frequent than clay models. The most primitive style of pole figure shows hyenas, illustrated by Routledge from among the Kikuyu (Routledge, 1910, Pl. 80). Wood-carving was rare even among the Pare. Gutmann says that wooden figures of human beings exist among the southern Pare as objects of worship (Gutmann, p. 17), but Baumann, who had close contact with the Pare, writes that the only human likenesses that he saw were wooden stoppers of gourd bottles used as a hiding place for magic symbols. These stoppers had crudely carved spherical human heads with flat faces and incised details (O. Baumann, 1891, pp. 240–1).

Roughly carved wooden figures were used by the Pare at initiation ceremonies for boys and girls. But only one of those published (Cory, 1956, pp. 143–6) represents a human figure, roughly outlined, with highly geometrical stylization.

It appears that, like the Pare, the Kahe had stick-shaped vessel stoppers with carved human heads (plate 52).

In recent times the Kamba have begun to carve little wooden figures, mainly intended for sale to Europeans. They first turned to this activity in the period of the first world war (Kjersmeier, Pl. 28; Trowell, p. 2; Elkan; Tracey).

An interesting collection of wood-carvings of the Chaga tribe is to be found in the ethnographical museum in Budapest. The statuettes, collected in the years 1902–3, were made, according to the collector, by a wood-carver who had previously made only wooden dishes, stools, etc., but never figures. All the wooden figures in Budapest today were made at the collector's suggestion (Vajda, 1955, p. 181). It is, in other words, an example of the skill of an individual craftsman, though it fully deserves attention.

The wooden sculptures of the Chaga can be divided into three groups. The first consists of animal figures (plate 53) carved of tree branches, whose natural shape were used for the composition. Some of these sculptures were enhanced with pokerwork.

The second group comprises sculptures depicting Africans (plate 54). As in the case of the first group they show a striving towards realism. Certain elements are typical of primitive sculptures in East Africa; the cylindrical body, spherical head, legs wide apart and thickening at the feet and calves. Though it is known that these figures were the work of one craftsman attempting figure carving, it is difficult to overlook the striking similarity to sculptures such as those of Sukuma, Kerewe and Nyasa.

The third group of Chaga figures in the Budapest museum comprises statues of missionaries and nuns (plate 55). They show a certain stylization and resemble the *nungu* clay figures closely, being cylindrical, widening at the bottom, with short stumps of arms alongside the body, and a spherical head with a crudely modelled face. The eyes and ears in the form of holes are very similar to those on the *nungu* figures. Vajda points out that this similarity is due to both groups being endowed with supernatural power or depicting beings that, in the eyes of the natives, were likewise bearers of certain supernatural powers (Vajda, 1955, p. 189).

The small carved wooden figures of the Chaga are mentioned by Trowell, who does not deal with their form or style (Trowell, p. 2).

# THE COASTAL STRIP OF THE INDIAN OCEAN

The coastal strip of Kenya and Tanzania is inhabited by a number of tribes who, since the first Arab invasions during the ninth century, have been strongly exposed to the cultural influence of the Arab world. Their present culture is a conglomerate of mainly Arab-Persian features. Sculpture has no place in it, and all art takes the form of rich ornamentation.

The Bantu tribes living inland differ greatly from the inhabitants of the coastal strip, the *watu wa mrima*, particularly in their culture. But even they show certain Arabic influences that penetrated from the coast. This is found only in the families of chiefs, who derived their origin from the Persian-Arab inhabitants of the coast, or in certain trade centres. The actual culture of the agricultural tribes in the villages is purely African. In their art the individual tribes living inland have specific qualities wherein they differ from the coastal inhabitants who lack all art, and from the artistically not very highly developed Bantu to the north-east.

Geographically and ethnographically, the Shambala represent a transition between the north-eastern Bantu and the tribes inhabiting the lowland areas along the shores of the Indian Ocean. About 80,000 Shambala live in the highlands of Usambara in north-eastern Tanzania. They are skilled craftsmen, and wood-carving is one of their subsidiary means of income. They have even developed a certain specialization in producing various wooden vessels and tools. Among their products special attention should be paid to wooden gourd-stoppers with ornamentally carved heads. There is a great variety of these stoppers—some have simple spherical or cudgel-shaped heads, others are more complex, with clear profiles. Stoppers for vessels and horns serving as hiding places for magic potions usually end in a carved human head, egg-shaped with a slightly concave face, with a broad nose, incised eyes, and a mouth indicated by a deep groove (plate 57). The stoppers serve to drive away evil spirits while the patient is anointed with a medicament from the bottle, and decorative chains of seeds and cowrie shells are used in sooth-saying (Karasek, Vol. VII, p. 79; Vol. VII, p. 35). Sticks sometimes have their handles with carved ornamental bird figures with long beaks (Karasek, Vol. I, p. 173).

The Shambala also carved figures of human beings. The female figure in the Linden-Museum in Stuttgart (plate 56) has an angular trunk with natural curves of the body widening at the hip and stiffness avoided by the bent knees and arms. The head, too, is carved in angular style. Another well-known Shambala figure, published by Fagg (Fagg, Pl. 97), is identical with this in basic principles of movement but stresses a softer curved line, more like Makonde sculpture. A wooden statue depicting a standing man is published by Karasek (Karasek, Vol. VIII, Pl. VI, fig. 242). This figure belongs to the *vizulu* type of sculpture (see below). It is roughly modelled and stiff, its only movement indicated in the bent arms.

The Shambala stools (plate 58) have typical highly stylized zoomorphic features, resembling the work of the Ngindo (H. Baumann, p. 128).

The Shambala were likewise skilled potters and used clay for modelling. A comparatively large number of pipes with human heads exist, also human and animal statues of black, roughly baked clay covered on the surface with graphite. According to Stuhlmann, these clay sculptures began to be made only under missionary influence. Karasek, however, is of the opinion that the European influence is to be felt only in a certain group of naturalistically conceived clay sculptures. He considers the *vizulu* sculptures as purely autochthonic; they were used in curing the sick, especially in serious cases (Stuhlmann, pp. 108–9; Karasek, Vol. VII, pp. 74 ff.).

An independent, likewise autochthonic group of clay sculptures of the Shambala is to be found in figurines used during initiation ceremonies for boys and girls, as in the case of the Pare. They were made by men and women, who organized the initiation ceremonies or even by participants at the ceremonies among the adults. The figurines were placed in the initiation hut and during the ceremony were shown

23

to the young boys or girls—together with the songs that accompanied each one—as aids which were to help them to understand the social values in their tribe. At the end of the ceremony they were always destroyed by being immersed in water (Cory, 1956). These little clay statues were crudely marked and only roughly modelled. They have stout cylindrical bodies, cylindrical legs and arms and a spherical head attached rather clumsily to the trunk. Usually the face was only roughly indicated: holes instead of eyes and a sharp-edged nose. Quite often the figures showed action or movement (for example, a sitting figure, an archer) (Cory, 1956, p. 46, Pl. 10), a kneeling figure, a rider on an elephant, etc. Clay animal figures were usually greatly stylized. They represent birds, hares, etc. Realistic depiction of animals is very rare. The animals are also caught in action, for example, a cat with her prey in her teeth (Cory, 1956, p. 44, Pl. 8).

The last group of Shambala clay statues, the *vinyuwa*, are obviously of more recent origin, as shown not only by their profane subject-matter, but the more perfect, clearly realistic form of the small statuettes. They generally depict men, with simple movements, or in more complex actions, for example, a man pulling a thorn out of his leg (Karasek, Vol. VII, p. 75, Pl. 193). Busts depicting natives are frequent.

Another tribe among the coastal Bantu that produced interesting sculpture are the Zaramo, living in the lowlands of the coastal strip of eastern Tanzania north of the Rufiji river. Their clothing, dwellings and tools show strong Arab influence, typical of the East African coast. On the other hand, the religious images of the Zaramo, to which their art is closely related, is of purely African character. The strong persistence of these purely African elements in an environment with a predominantly Arab and Islamic culture led some investigators to think that the Zaramo originated further west (for example, Stuhlmann, pp. 32–3).

The first group of Zaramo wooden sculpture are figures placed on graves, which in form do not differ from Moslem graves. These tomb figures with long cylindrical, superficially modelled bodies have movable arms and legs, and the head with its slightly concave face is usually wrapped in a cloth turban. The general appearance of these Zaramo tomb figures is slightly comical (Fagg, Pl. 98).

Another type of Zaramo sculpture includes magic wands called *tambiko*, with figures carved at the end (plate 59); in general, they resemble Shambala sticks in slightly simplified form. The *tambiko* are used as normal walking sticks, but play a role in curing children. If the child is ill, the medicine man tries first to discover the cause of the illness by drawing in the sand. In the actual process of treatment, the child grasps his father's stick in his hand, and believes that the magic power of the stick will return his good health. The ends of war horns, and the ridges and sides of wooden tobacco cases are decorated with figure carvings similar to those on the sticks.

A third type of figure carving found among the Zaramo is the *mwana kiti*. These are wooden dolls carried by unmarried girls and married women until the birth of the first child (plates 60–61). These puppets have the basic shape of a cylinder, a truncated cone and spherical segment. The interplay of those shapes produces the appearance of a puppet. The cubist conception of these figures is joined to a naturalistic endeavour to enhance the head by the addition of plant fibres to indicate hair (Stuhlmann, p. 32; Reckling, pp. 31–7; H. Baumann, p. 196; von Sydow, p. 102).

24

Apart from wooden sculptures, the Zaramo also have clay statuettes, differing very little in style from the clay figures of the Shambala and other tribes along the shores of the Indian Ocean. Like the other tribes of this group they use them for boys' initiation ceremonies (Cory, 1956, p. 172).

Carved dolls—*mwana kiti*—are known also among the Doei tribe, living further inland from the coastal Zaramo (plate 62). The Doei dolls are identical in shape to those of the Zaramo. Only the face with concave grooves has different plastic details.

Figures of human beings are also made by the Bondei, living next to the Shambala and Zaramo in north-eastern Tanzania (plate 63). The carvings are largely reminiscent of the tomb sculptures of the Zaramo—a cylindrical body on massive legs, with short stiff arms, bearing a head with a faintly concave face, with the features shown in shallow detail.

We also know certain clay sculptures from the Zigula, the southern neighbours of the Shambala and Bondei, very similar to the Shambala ones. They also are used during initiation ceremonies for boys and girls (Cory, 1956). Parts of the stylized clay sculptures of the Zigula stress certain realistic features, for example, the hairstyle, and the face is usually much more sculptural than on the Shambala clay figures. They depict certain actions, for example, bending down, raising of arms, etc. The clay animal figures made by that tribe are almost identical with those of the Shambala. Sometimes paint was used to decorate the statuettes.

The Nguru, of whom a mere 18,000 live in the hilly areas to the west and south-west of the Zigula territory, also make clay figures, which are used for the same initiation ceremonies (Cory, 1944, 1947, 1948, 1956). Their figures depicting human beings are fairly stylized. Some (for example, Cory, 1956, p. 102, Pl. 90) are almost identical with Chaga sculptures (plate 45). Most of the figures have stylized cylindrical bodies with arms and head shown by small projections, and usually without legs. The modelling of the face is usually almost non-existent. Figural compositions of figures in action are not as frequent as among the Shambala and Zigula. The animal figures found among the Nguru art are similar to those of the Shambala and Zigula.

Gravestone sculpture, which has an analogy in south-west Ethiopia is known among the coastal Bantu tribes of Giriama and Nyika in south-east Kenya.

The Giriama have two types of gravestones, situated either on the graves or at some important place in the village itself. The first type, called *koma* is not very interesting from an artistic point of view and takes the form of short poles depicting the deceased. The second type, called *vigango*, is found among richer families. The *vigango* are flat wooden poles, about 1.50 metres (5 feet) tall, 21 centimetres ($8\frac{1}{4}$ inches) wide and 4.7 centimetres ($1\frac{7}{8}$ inches) thick, ornamented sometimes with simple geometrical designs, and others ending in more realistic carvings of human heads. The *vigango*, like the *koma*, are likenesses of the dead (Barrett, p. 24).

Analogous grave-poles are also to be found among the neighbouring Nyika. There, too, they depict the dead, but carved human heads are rare. The Nyika try to express the likeness to the deceased by using parts of his garments, which they wrap round the poles (Hollis, p. 145, Werner, p. 343).

Among the group of tribes, generally called Nyika, there lives, alongside the Nyika proper and the Giriama, the small Bantu tribe of the Eile, living in the river valley of the Shebelle in Somaliland, where their culture does not greatly differ from that of the surrounding Somali, and the Bantu tribe of the Gosha, living along the lower reaches of the Juba river: their culture has fully merged with that of the Somali Sab tribe, on whose territory they are living. The Eile and Gosha carve artistically remarkable masks used at dance ceremonies in rain-making, curing of ill persons and infertile women (Clark, pp. 49–51). Their masks are examples of the most easterly spread of wood-carving in north-east Africa.

## SOUTHERN TANZANIA

Atransitional stage of art between the tribes living along the coast of Tanzania and those in Mozambique can be found among the Ngindo and the Mwera living to the east along the coast; their neighbours to the south are the Makindo of Mozambique.

We possess Ngindo masks (plate 64) and zoomorphic stools (plate 65). In conception the Ngindo masks fall within the primitive style known among the Shilluk, Ziba and other East African tribes. They tend to be flat and only nose and ears project from the smooth block. Eyes and mouth are indicated by apertures. The forehead and chin bear simple engraved ornaments. Far more expressive and more perfect in form are the stools in stylized zoomorphic shapes. The stylization is given by the function of the object, though a likeness to the animal portrayed is achieved. Characteristic features include carved geometrical ornaments which cover the entire stool.

More striking parallels to the woodcarvings of the Makonde can be found in the work of the Mwera tribe. They are usually described as statues of ancestors. Some Mwera sculptures represent the evil spirit *mchipira*, whom the Mwera consider the cause of most illnesses; they depicted it in human form with short stumps instead of the left leg and arm and only one eye and ear. The wooden statues of the Mwera, by contrast to the work of other East African tribes, show a certain skill in handling plastic form and indicating movement. The head, trunk and limbs do not constitute a undivided block but are conceived as mutually interconnected mobile forms. Similarly the treatment of facial features is more advanced. These traits link them with the Makonde-style figures but, in overall concept, they do not reach the high qualities of that style (von Sydow, p. 105).

The Mwera masks, too (plates 66–67), contain some of the features of the Makonde masks. The facial parts are curved and naturalistic, and the features of the face reveal a feeling for form. Simplification appears only in the eye holes and modelling of the mouth.

Wooden sculpture is known among certain other of the south Tanzanian tribes: the Matumbi, the western neighbours of the Ngindo, the Pangwo, living on the Livingstone Mountains north-east of Lake Nyasa, and the Matengo, living to the south on the borders of Mozambique. In principle, they are identical to the sculptures of the Mwera, but simpler in form. The concave faces are striking in all of them. We know the purpose of the wooden statuettes of the Matengo: they were carried by childless women (von Sydow, p. 106).

It appears that wooden sculpture did not exist among the fishing tribe of the Kissi along the north-eastern shores of Lake Nyasa. The Kissi women were however, skilful potters, whose wares were sold far afield, and clay seems to have been the main material in which they produced figurines. The clay sculpture of the Kissi (plate 68) took the form of highly stylized, roughly modelled dolls with long cylindrical bodies merging with the heads and short legs. The faces lack almost all details.

Clay figures are also known among the Bena tribe in southern Tanzania (Richards, 1956, p. 9).

The southern part of East Africa includes the territory of Mozambique and that of north-eastern Zambia and Malawi. Here live numerous tribes with distinct forms of sculpture. The wooden figure carvings and masks of the tribes in northern Mozambique certainly represent the climax of art on East African soil.

The area of northern Mozambique, to be more precise that between Lake Nyasa and the Indian Ocean—called 'Lindi-Hinterland' in German literature—is inhabited by the Makonde, Mawia and Yao tribes (plates 69–106). The perfection of their art, at first sight, clearly surpasses the far more primitive art of East Africa. Their work is similar to that of the Congo and Western Sudan, which is usually labelled the 'West African' style. While up to now the principal features in the East African region have been stiffness, angularity and disproportion, now for the first time we meet free movement, curves and soft shapes with balanced proportions in various degrees of perfection.

The best known of the tribes of northern Mozambique are the Makonde, a small number of whom live on the northern banks along the lower reaches of the Rovuma river, which forms the frontier between Mozambique and Tanzania. They are farmers who own no cattle and keep only small domestic animals. Their wooden sculpture show women at rest (plates 77, 81, 85) or, occasionally, in dance movements (plates 78–9). All Makonde sculpture shows the artist's endeavour to achieve a realistic depiction of the human figure, often close to naturalism and exaggerated caricature. The bodies are modelled in natural proportions with balanced curved lines and the centre of gravity is lowered as the result of bent knees. Greatest attention is devoted to the head. The eyes are set in shallow holes contrasting sharply with the protruding lip plugs in the upper lip. The arms are always slightly bent, hanging down the curves of the body or are folded across the abdomen. In the case of dancing figures the arms are bent at the height of the chest. The colour of the figures is reddish or blackish, and where scarification is shown it is outlined in black.

We do not know the exact significance of the carved female figures. We owe our basic information on the Makonde culture to the German ethnologist Weule, who collected the greatest number of examples of their art, found today in the museum in Leipzig. He describes the carvers as being inspired by their wish to depict remarkable faces and methods of tattooing. He thinks, however, that the female figures must have been cult figures representing the primaeval matriarch-founder of the tribe (Weule, 1908a, pp. 49 ff.). A similar view is held by Adam, who says that the function of the wooden female figures must have been to recall the mythological creation of the first woman, the founder of the tribe. According to the myth that the statues illustrate, the first man carved a wooden statue and placed it in his hut. During the night the statue came to life and became his mate who gave birth to the first Makonde (Adam, p. 44).

Besides the statues, the most expressive works of art made by the Makonde are masks (plates 76, 86–101, 104). They depict men and women, usually famous warriors. The masks with long horns and beards are portraits of the devil (plate 99). Even masks of animals exist. They were used during dance ceremonies, held as part of the initiation ceremonies for girls. Young men dressed in the masks performed dances. Apart from masks over their faces the dancers representing women carried wooden boards on their chest with carved breasts, belly, and scarification marked in beeswax (plate 91). The

Leipzig museum owns one female mask on which the face and tablet covering the breast and abdomen are carved out of one piece of wood (von Sydow, p. 105). The central motive of the masked dancers was a dramatic representation of sexual intercourse. The dancers with male and female masks danced in pairs facing one another. Only the lower part of their bodies moved while the arms and legs remained motionless. Some masks were used for dances during initiation ceremonies, particularly some male masks and others representing animals and even the devil, which aimed at causing terror and fear (Weule, 1908a, pp. 111 ff., p. 444; Germann, 1958, p. 54).

The Makonde masks can be divided into two groups. The first does not greatly differ from those found on East African territory in general. They are circular or oval in outline, slightly convex with very flat modelling. The eyes take the shape of slits cut into concave parts out of which a sharply edged nose protrudes. Some masks show scarification; in some masks the wooden lip-plug distorting the upper lip is clearly shown while the male masks are fringed with beards. Most animal masks and many male and female ones belong to this first group. One Makonde mask in the Linden-Museum in Stuttgart is particularly interesting: a sitting wooden figure is placed on a face mask of the type described (von Sydow, Pl. 142D, E). All these masks are face masks.

The second group has a typical circular, curved style, like the free-standing sculpture, and there is a leaning towards naturalism and grotesque caricature. These masks, known as helmet masks, are hollow, carved in the round, and are designed to be worn on top of the head. They have softer lines and show more faithful portrayal. On the male masks hair is indicated by skin or hair, beards by grass or hair. The faces show scarification and they have protruding upper lips, distorted by lip-plugs. Some masks increased their effect by the polychromy of red colour contrasting with the black hair and scarification.

There is no sharp division between the two groups of masks, as some of them bear characteristics of both types. One of the most beautiful among the Makonde masks is to be found in the Linden-Museum in Stuttgart (plate 97). The Makonde made not only human figures and carved masks but also statuettes of animals and birds (Weule, 1908a, Pl. 22) and poles with ornamental figures (plate 105).

The clay figures of the Makonde stand in striking contrast to the perfection of their wood carving. The small clay figurine of a bull (plate 103) served as a toy as among other East African tribes.

The Mawia tribe, belonging to the group of Makonde tribes has a similar artistic style (plate 106).

The Yao, living in the western parts of northern Mozambique and southern Tanzania and Malawi, make helmet masks stylistically reminiscent of those of the Makonde second-group masks (plate 102), with naturalistic leanings and grotesque caricature. The curved softly modelled heads with flat protruding forehead and broad flat noses have the typical protruding lips and well shaped narrow eyes and ears.

The figure carvings of the Yao, according to Stannus, are of more recent origin and are the result of contact with the Europeans. Wooden sculptures representing natives, Europeans, antelopes, leopards and other animals were all exclusively intended for sale to foreigners. The Yao do not make any wood-carvings for their own use for fear of black magic. Their only autochthonous carvings are small figures of birds sometimes used to adorn the roofs of their houses (Stannus, 1922, p. 348).

Unique in Yao art are clay reliefs mainly representing animals of various kinds, and certain other objects, such as the moon, Lake Nyasa, etc. They serve during boys' initiation ceremonies (unyago), during which they are used to give the initiates various information about their future life (Stannus and Davey, pp. 119–23; Stannus, 1922, pp. 260, 265 ff.).

The tribe's westerly neighbours, the Makua, likewise use clay figures during girls' initiation ceremonies (Cory, 1956, p. 172).

## THE TERRITORY TO THE WEST AND SOUTH OF LAKE NYASA

Among the tribes of north-eastern Zambia the most expressive art is to be found among the Bemba (plate 107). The figure in the Horniman Museum in London shows all the features typical of the pole style of East African sculpture. The cylindrical body is widened at the hips and stands on narrow pillar-shaped legs, the thin angular arms follow the lines of the trunk and are bent at the elbow. Decorative scarification is shown on the chest, abdomen and face. The features on the concave face are shallow and linear.

The Bemba also produce clay figurines, which, according to Richards and Schofield, are related in style to the sculpture found in Zimbabwe. They are used during girls' initiation ceremonies.

This was likewise the purpose of clay models found among the Nyamwanga, the north-eastern neighbours of the Bemba, who live on Tanzanian territory (Cory, 1956, p. 172).

The Bisa, the Bemba's southern neighbours, make masks (Stannus, 1910, p. 298), though unfortunately, we have no exact information about their appearance. Masks are also produced by the Chewa, living east of the Bisa on the western shores of Lake Nyasa (Rangley), and by the Mambwe, the Bemba's northern neighbours living on the borders between northern Zambia and Tanzania (plate 109). They closely resemble those made by the Ziba, and are oval in shape, comparatively flat with a clearly protruding nose and with teeth set in the rectangular mouth opening. Their eyes are shown as simple square holes.

One mask from north-eastern Zambia, without exact provenance, is to be found in the Musée de l'Homme in Paris (plate 108). It is flat and circular, with fur along the edges. The cylindrical nose and the horizontal stripes on the forehead give it plasticity. The eyes have the shape of narrow slits. The effect is heightened by the alternation of light and dark cross-wise lines.

The tribes living on the territory south of Lake Nyasa also produce works of art. The British Museum possesses a wooden sculpture of a woman carrying a child on her back. It came from the Blantyre area in southern Malawi, together with two other figures (plates 110–112). These figures are similar to those made by the Bemba tribe. The body is cylindrical with stick-like legs wide apart, simply modelled, often with short arms. In contrast to the Bemba figures they have no decorative scars. Typical features are the rather brutal expression on the faces, and the use of animal skin to represent hair.

The Lomwe have a style of carving of their own. They are a fairly large tribe living partly in Malawi and partly in Mozambique territory south-east of Lake Nyasa. The Berlin Museum owns two sculptures from Lake Shirwa on the border between Malawi and Mozambique (plates 113–14). They differ in conception: the first (plate 113) has a short body with broad hips and rather long massive legs modelled naturalistically. The short arms lie across the abdomen. In proportion to the figure the head is large. The figure is bending slightly forwards, and is stabilized by its outsize feet. In the second figure (plate 114) a strictly vertical principle is adhered to. The extended cylindrical body and elongated arms bent at the elbow and lying on the abdomen are in balance. The legs are shortened. These two figures have similar engraved geometrical decorations covering body and legs, and concave faces with protruding lips.

The Chemba tribe in the area south-east of Lake Shirwa is represented in two wooden masks belonging to the Stuttgart Museum (plate 116). In appearance they are strikingly similar to some of the masks of the first Makonde group. The concave parts of the face are divided into two halves by the sharp-edged nose, the eyes and mouth are marked by holes, and similarity can also be found in the beeswax decorations on the face.

Masks exist also among the Chuabo, living on the territory along the lower reaches of the Zambezi river. They are used for boys' and girls' initiation ceremonies when they are worn by the elders, both men and women, who are in charge of the ceremony. The masks used for girls' ceremonies are white, the colour of the dead. The dancers, who wear both male and female masks, act out funeral scenes in them (von Sydow, p. 106).

The Nyanja, living to the north-east of the Chuabo, carve magic wands as protection against illness, stools and carved figurines of birds as ornaments on pipes (H. Baumann, pp. 125–6, 138). Even though these sculptures are determined by the function of the objects they adorn, which restricts them, it appears that of all the tribes these have the greatest feeling for geometrical stylization.

Their black wooden face masks, which have also been published, have rather flat, sharply protruding, long noses, slits for eye holes and grooves along the forehead and cheeks. They are surrounded by a wreath of hair and a long beard. They are worn by dancers doing the zinyao dance at the end of girls' initiation ceremonies (Metcalfe, pp. 687–9). Apart from woodcarvings the Nyanja also make clay figures used on the same occasions (Germann, 1958, p. 38).

The groups of tribes living along the lower reaches of the Zambezi and in Malawi, among which the Chuabo and Nyanja must be counted, are generally known as the Maravi. This is the label given to a standing female figure in the Berlin Museum (plate 115). It has a long body, bent legs wide apart and plastically modelled arms lying on the abdomen. The spherical head is rather small, and the face is modelled in shallow relief. The trunk and head are ornamented to represent scarification. As a whole the figure in its posture recalls some of the sculptures of the Makonde, Bemba, and Lomwe. It is linked to the work of the two latter tribes by the geometrical decoration on the body.

In this part mention will be made of the art of the tribes living in the vast expanses of the African continent to the south of the Zambezi.

One of the African tribes whose art is similar in style to sculptures found in the ruins of Zimbabwe are the Rotse, or more correctly, the Lozi, living along the middle reaches of the river Zambezi on the territory of Zambia. This similarity in style is to be seen in figures of birds that form the capitals of columns found at Zimbabwe (Bent, fig. on p. 151; Hall, figs. on pp. 348, 352, 364; Caton-Thompson, Pl. 51; Frobenius 1931, Pl. 51). Such bird figures are used as decorations on lids of wooden food dishes. Other figures found on these lids include lions, antelopes, fishes, human beings, riders, etc. (plates 117, 119, 121). Besides these realistically portrayed figures exist others with a high degree of stylization (plate 118).

The statuettes of the Rotse are not of a unified style. The small horn sculpture (plate 123), belonging to a private collection in Belgium, still has certain features of the pole-figures. The robust figure with a cylindrical trunk and a small spherical head on which facial features are given only superficially, has carefully shaped legs, while the arms are given in clumsy form in an endeavour to portray movement. The sculpture of a kneeling figure (plate 122) holding a dish in its hands shows the influence of the Lunda style. The well-balanced body has natural curves of movements and the rounded forms are dominant in the whole and in details. Geometrical ornaments are used on the body, as among the Bemba, Lomwe and Maravi.

Masks are of two types: the first is made of painted bast with rays of ornaments on the tall broad forehead, which projects above the flat face. The nose, short narrow lips and eyebrows form hollows on the face. The second type of mask is made of wood with broad arched forehead and broad nose. The cheeks are convex and the open mouth has protruding lips.

The Lozi also carved animal figures into headrests and stools (plate 120). They show the same features as the wooden dishes. Carved animal figures are used as ornaments on other objects of daily use, for example, on spoons (H. Baumann, p. 133).

Other forms of art among the Lozi include bird and animal carvings in ivory, which in the view of some authors shows an analogy to the Zimbabwe sculptures (Trevor, p. 329). They also produce clay figurines made by children as toys (Holub, Vol. II, p. 388; Christol, pp. 111 ff.).

The Mbunda, who used to be part of the Rotse empire on the middle Zambezi, made masks. They were used during *makishi* dances, held by the Mbunda every fortnight at Shesheke, the capital of the Rotse empire. They were made by children out of clay and cattle dung and when used for the dances coloured red and white with ochre and lime. (Holub, Vol. II, pp. 197 ff.; Frobenius, 1898, Pl. 2, figs. 3–4.) The Mbunda also possessed wooden masks. Fagg (Elisofon and Fagg, p. 251) published as 'Mbunda masks used at makishi dances' a wooden mask which is identical with masks attributed to the Subia tribe, living on the middle Zambezi to the south of the Rotse (plate 124). The masks attributed to the Subia by von Sydow and others are now attributed to the Mbunda by J. D. Clark, formerly director of the Rhodes-Livingstone Museum. The shape is oval, convex with a rounded arched forehead with shallow grooves following the line of the eyebrows, a broad nose and projecting mouth of rectangular or segmented shape with two rows of teeth. Around the forehead the masks usually have a crest of feathers.

This similarity in style does not only apply to the masks but also to wooden food dishes with lids with ornamental figures (H. Baumann, p. 130). Like the Lozi they use both the naturalistic principle and certain attempts at stylization.

The Totela, living to the west of the Rotse and south of the Subia, carve figural headrests (plate 125). The example in the British Museum shows a figure supporting the headrest. The body is cylindrical with stumps of arms close to it. The head with superficial modelling of the face sits on a long neck.

The Ila, living a little further east on the middle Zambezi, make clay pipes in the shape of animals (H. Baumann, p. 131). They are organically composed as part of the body of the animal depicted.

The art of the Zezuru in Rhodesia, like that of the Lozi along the middle Zambezi, is closely related to Zimbabwe art. This analogy applies to zoomorphic clay dishes (plates 126–8). The one in the Frankfurt museum (plate 127) is almost identical with such vessels found at Zimbabwe (for example, Frobenius, 1931, p. 274). The vessels were made in the shape of stylized animal bodies on short legs, with cylindrical, slightly widened necks. They gain in effect by the alternation of triangular red and black areas all over the vessel.

Among Zezuru wood-carvings must be counted masks (plate 129). They are almost identical with those produced by the Mbunda. The mask with two horns in the collection of the Hamburg Museum is likewise oval, slightly convex with typical grooved forehead. The broad nose is carved in sharp lined edges and a similar sharp line can be found along the ridge of the nose and the lines leading from the root of the nose to the cheekbones. The eyes are narrow slits like the Rotse and Subia masks.

The first of the tribes where works of art are produced are the Venda, whose 135,000 inhabitants live in northern Transvaal. Some authors consider that their culture is related to that of the Shona tribes living in Rhodesia and adjacent parts of Mozambique. The Shona tribes, among them the Zezuru, are often considered to be tribes that must have been in very close contact with the Zimbabwe culture, if not its direct descendants. This view would be upheld by some of the carvings of the Venda, in particular soapstone oracle dishes, which are reminiscent of such dishes found at Zimbabwe (H. Baumann, p. 122). Along the narrow edge of the circular dishes are carved small stylized animal and human figures, set along a strip with symbolic marks. In the centre of the dishes are likewise stylized animal figures and symbolic marks, set in rays emerging from the centre.

The actual Venda woodcarvings are basically of the style of the pole figures of East Africa. Some of them belong to the Berlin Museum. Most of them are carved out of light-coloured wood without any striking style. The same applies to headrests made by the Venda (von Sydow, pp. 108–9).

The Venda, like the Lovedu, their south-eastern neighbours, and the Ndau, living in southern Mozambique to the north of the Thonga tribes, make clay figures used during initiation ceremonies (Richards, 1956, p. 9).

The Venda carvings are similar in style to the sculpture of the Thonga tribes, with whom they form one ethnic group, living mainly on the territory of southern Mozambique south-east of the Shona tribes. There are roughly one million of them. Some authors believe that the Thonga adopted wood-carving from the Venda (Walk, p. 910). The Tonga carvings are of secular character. For one of the group of Thonga tribes, the Ronga, we have concrete proof that they own no ancestor figures, although the ancestor cult is highly developed among them (Junod, Vol. II, p. 347).

Although certain figures made by the Thonga are exhibited in various European museums, attribution to particular tribes remains problematic. It would seem that the majority of the Thonga carvings come from the Shanga, immigrant Nguni living among the aboriginal Thonga. Some of their sculptures belong to the Berlin collections. In style they are pole figures with clearly elongated cylindrical bodies, long limbs and a small head. The hips are covered by loin cloths of cotton or beads (von Sydow, p. 107). The figures in Vienna are more lively and show leanings towards naturalism.

Wooden figures are also known among the Mindonga, living in the south of Mozambique north of the river Limpopo. Two figures made by that tribe of the Thonga group belong to the Museum für Völkerkunde in Basle. The female figure shows tattooing on the chin, abdomen and back which are more ornamental than the similar marks on her male companion. We possess no information as to the significance of these works (von Sydow, p. 107).

The Rijksmuseum voor Volkenkunde at Leyden possesses among its collections some statues of light-coloured wood marked as Nguni/Thonga (plates 130–1, 133–4). Most of the figures represent pairs of male and female figures with long cylindrical trunks and limbs. The cylindrical modelling is interrupted with the aim of introducing more naturalistic forms of the human body, but is never completely consistent. The heads are mostly disproportionately small compared with the prolonged line of the figures, and are spherical, with eyes and mouth in shallow relief. The male figures usually have a head-ring. Similar formal aspects are found among Thonga figures published by Junod (Junod, p. 118). They represent secular subjects: natives dressed in European garments and a woman with a child on her back. Not even the garment hides the cylindrical shape of the figure. These figurines with strongly grotesque features, like the one of the leopard devouring an Englishman, are modern works of Mowumbi carvers.

Objects of everyday use are likewise covered with figures, mainly sticks with human heads or carvings of male figures standing on the heads of female figures. Figural motives appear also on spoons and ladles (Junod, Vol. II, pp. 111, 117).

Related to Thonga figures are works by the Zulu of the Nguni group, likewise to be found in the Rijksmuseum voor Volkenkunde (plates 135–7). These figures, too, have cylindrical bodies, with some attempt at more natural modelling in the case of a few of them. The male figures are again adorned with head-rings. There is a striking female Zulu figure to be found in the Vienna Museum (plate 138). The powerful arch of the shoulders is balanced by a mighty arch of the strong legs, slightly bent at the knees. In comparison with other parts the trunk is very slim. The small spherical head with large ears has a short strong nose and open mouth, which slightly protrudes out of the level of the face. The construction of the body is similar to Rotse bone figures. If the attribution to the Zulu is correct, it must be assumed that we are dealing with a modern work, made for sale. The figural carving on a headrest makes an equally modern impression (plate 140), mainly in its animal motives.

The South African statuettes in the Musée de l'Homme are assumed by von Sydow to be recent works, also meant for sale to foreigners. They are attributed to the Pondo, another tribe of the Nguni group who live to the south of the Zulu. Typical of these sculptures are their naive naturalistic tendencies.

The subject-matter of the Zulu carvings seems to indicate their recent origin: uniformed riders on horseback, a train, a merry-go-round, etc. (Battiss, pp. 130–1). It would, therefore, appear that the traditional culture of the Nguni tribes did not include figure sculptures which existed only among the northernmost Thonga (H. Baumann, p. 116). The Nguni made only wooden bowls, headrests and sticks endings in either human heads or human and animal figures, sometimes decorated elsewhere with bas-reliefs of human or animal figures (plate 139) (Battis, pp. 125–30).

The Zulu also produced clay figures. They served as toys and were often made by the children themselves. Most frequently they represent bulls, but human figures are to be found, for example, the clay statue of a man, drinking from a cup, a small statue of a woman and child, or one of a rider on horseback (Battiss, p. 124). Clay dolls were made as children's toys. Their bodies and even heads were covered or hung with strings of glass beads (plates 141, 142). Where the face was not covered with these beads it was flatly modelled and facial details were rarely shown. They may, however, not have been toys but symbols bringing women fertility, or serving as protection for the child.

The Nguni tribes are artistically close to the Sotho and Tswana tribes, living in Basutoland and large inland territories in the Union of South Africa and in Bechuanaland. They made zoomorphic or figure carvings on headrests, their sticks ended in carved standing figures, spoons had handles with ornamental animal figures, wooden bowls had lids with ornamental figures, and they made separate small carvings in wood of animals and birds. (Christol, pp. 52, 93, 94; H. Baumann, pp. 115–6). The age of these sculptures is highly problematic and they may well have come into being by the potential possibilities of sale to Europeans.

Clay was also used. Dried clay or terra-cotta pieces include bird-shaped bowl (Christol, pp. 55, 68) and clay animal figures with which Sotho children play (plates 143, 145, 146). Some figures exist only in rough outlines while others with careful modelling attempted a truthful depiction of the subject.

The Sotho, like the Zulu, also have clay dolls (plates 147, 149), worn by childless women on their backs. The little bodies were wrapped in cloth or sewn into strings of beads, with head modelling similar to those of the Zulu.

Similar wooden or clay dolls are known among the Ambo in the northern parts of South-West Africa (plates 148, 150, 152). Some of the dolls are highly stylized. The middle part is covered in beads, the spherical head rarely includes any facial features.

Wooden headrests are carved in the shape of animal figures (plate 151). This is the only form of sculpture among the Ambo apart from the primitive dolls.

This survey shows that East and South African sculpture lacks unity and presents a diversified picture. Even in places where we have been able to trace certain similarities of style and identity, we could not do so without any reservations. It is difficult to arrive at any conclusions and theories on related styles in East and South African sculpture on account of the uneven number of surviving examples among the various tribes and groups, the differences in material and other debatable points. Various, even contradictory elements of style merge in East Africa, disappearing only to re-emerge in other places. Where we have been able to discover identical features in, for example, masks, clay figures or stools within a certain region, they may well be related to a completely different area. Since the traditional East African forms of sculpture are today already a closed chapter in African history, it will become increasingly difficult to add new facts to our present knowledge.

The outward appearance of a sculpture cannot be the only guiding line giving clues to relations or styles. In such rudimentary forms of art similarity may well be accidental. In trying to find certain similarities or identical features we have to take into account other factors that might cause the similarity or have an influence to bear upon it, in particular the social function of the work of art.

Such similarity in style and function appears in ancestor figures, known among the Bari, Dinka, and Ingassana in the Sudan, and the Gato and their neighbours in south-western Ethiopia. The carvings of these tribes deserve in the full sense of the term the name 'pole sculpture'. Even if in some cases, particularly the Bari works, the image of the human figure is fully developed, the rudimentary pillar-shaped character of the figure and the static, stiff form with superficial modelling remains fully preserved. Elements of that style—if the word can be applied to such primitive forms of sculpture—are found among other tribes where it appears in slightly more advanced form (for example, the Bongo) or parallel with another form (Zaramo). Traces of the pole-style appear on certain figures of the Zande in the north-eastern Congo, the Sara and other tribes living further to the west of the Central Sudan. Where masks appear in the area of the pole style, they are all simple oval-shaped face masks with clear lines for the nose and square or circular holes for eyes and mouth (for example, the Shilluk).

In the remaining territories of East and South-East Africa the predominant form of sculpture is the type made most strikingly by the Thonga and Zulu. These sculptures have long, slim cylindrical bodies, stick-like arms and legs, and small spherical heads on which facial parts are marked only superficially. The vertical line is predominant in all sculpture of this type. Deviations from the basic form are not too clear or expressive. They are limited to certain methods of animation, achieved by bent arms or legs. Most typical of this style are the figures of the Kerewe, Sukuma and Nyasa and certain aspects are met with among the Nyamwezi, Hehe and Bemba. The figures of more recent origin made by the Chaga are also made in this manner. In this region of cylindrical figures masks can be divided into two groups. The first includes very simple face masks known among the group of tribes with pole-shaped figures, among them the masks of the Ziba, Iraku, Ngindo and Mambwe. Another type of mask is characterized by a wrinkled forehead and protruding and half-open, rectangular or oval-shaped mouth, in which teeth are indicated.

The rather limited production of sculpture among the Bondei, Mwera, Pangwa and Matengo give a more unified impression. The basic elements of these figures are likewise cylindrical, but are adapted to the natural lines, with detail indicating movement. They all have concave faces. This group of figures is, basically, linked with pole figures, but in regard to movement they are closer to the style of northern Mozambique, which in German literature bears the term 'Lindi-Hinterland'.

This area of northern Mozambique, chiefly inhabited by the tribes of the Makonde, Yao, and Mawia, represents a region unique in East African art. Part of their product links even these tribes to the art of the rest of East Africa. The interconnexion is clear from certain of their face masks, which are similar to the flat masks of the tribes with cylindrical figures, and some of their simplest works. But a very considerable part of their work, particularly the famous figures of dancing women and helmet masks intended to be worn on the top of the head have no analogy anywhere else in East Africa. The influence of the Makonde style can also be seen in Maravi works (plate 115). It is also noticeable in the Chemba masks. It remains to be determined to what extent the Makonde and other tribes of northern Mozambique form an enclave of the 'West African style' on East African territory or to what extent they represent the culmination of development of East African art as such.

Another problem that arises from an examination of the various samples we have had access to are the works of the Jiji, Bende, Lomwe and Lozi. The influence of foreign impulses, in particular from the Congo, is more than visible. Since, however, they are isolated examples of this art it is difficult to arrive at any conclusion for the time being.

The climax of stylized art in East Africa is found in the dolls, particularly those of the Doei and Zaramo. They reduce the human body into basic elements of cylinders and cones. By adding these into a composition and the intermingling of these elements an image of a human body is achieved. Similar trends can be found among the Sotho and Ambo, where cylinder and sphere serve as basic elements of structure.

A special chapter in East and South African art should be devoted to clay figures. They can be traced throughout the territory of East Africa. The tribes of the Chaga, Kikuyu, Pare, Shambala, Zaramo and their neighbours form the main centre of clay sculpture, but some are made by the Shilluk, Dinka, Vinza, Sukuma, Kissi, Sotho and several others. From a formal point of view East African clay figures are not particularly outstanding or interesting. They are all relatively similar, and are simple, roughly worked figures, often highly stylized (for example, Kissi, Chaga, etc.). Far more interesting than the form is the function of these figures, which is mostly closely related to religious or magic cults. In many tribes of East and South Africa children make such clay figures or they are made for children as toys.

## NORTHERN SUDAN

**1**   **Doll.  Omdurman.  Composite.**                    **h. 44 cm. British Museum, London.**
The head of this doll is modelled in camel dung, with pieces of grass stalk to represent facial tattooing. The fibre hair is dressed in small strands tipped with mud and ornamented with beads. The doll wears a cotton dress, and her wooden legs have metal anklets. This, and the three following dolls, are dressed to resemble native Sudanese Arab women as closely as possible; they may be toys, or made for sale to tourists, or to induce fertility.

**2**   **Doll.  Omdurman.  Composite.**                    **h. 44 cm. British Museum, London.**
This doll is made in similar manner to the first, but the photograph shows the hair and face in greater detail. The body and legs are made of sticks, the arms of stuffed cotton tubes.

**3**   **Doll.  Omdurman.  Composite.**                    **h. 33 cm. British Museum, London.**
This raffish looking doll has a finely moulded face and long hair dressed with clay and ornamented with glass beads and pearl buttons. The fibre skirt seems to have a long tasselled train, and the aluminium anklets are elaborately finished.

**4**   **Doll. Ed Dueim. Composite.**                    **h. 30 cm. Linden-Museum, Stuttgart.**
This doll's expressive face is unfortunately spoiled by worm holes, but the splendid clay-tipped coiffure and long bead necklace help to compensate. The long skirt is made of plain cotton cloth, and anklets, similar to those in plate 3, are visible. This, and the doll in plate 3, are probably about 30 years older than those in plates 1 and 2.

## SOUTHERN SUDAN

**5**   **Standing male figure. Ingassana tribe. Wood. h. 85.5 cm. British Museum, London.**
The slightly straddled legs help to give this carving a crude strength, despite its clumsy finish. The eyes are made of upholstery nails, the oval mouth has wooden pegs to represent teeth, some animal skin is stuck on the head for hair, and the loin-cloth is made of canvas. The body is coloured with red ochre. This is a reproduction of a figure called *tshalk* or *chalk*, which were wooden figures, possessed by certain players who functioned at marriage, the birth of twins, or the illness of children. The figures might be of a man or a woman or both, and also a wooden phallus, with which the *chalk* plays. The office is generally hereditary, but anyone who learns the dances may play (E. Evans-Pritchard, *Sudan Notes and Records*, 1927, Vol. X, p. 74).

**6**   **Leopard mask. Shilluk tribe. Gourd. h. 19 cm. Museum für Völkerkunde, Berlin.**
This circular, slightly convex mask is made of a piece of gourd daubed with cattle dung and with the ears and long, sharply ridged nose modelled in applied cattle dung. The eyes and mouth are shown by circular holes, and fish bones, of which only two remain, were stuck into the mouth for teeth.

**7ab**   **Hyena.  Shilluk tribe.  Baked clay.**                    **l. 16.3 cm. British Museum, London.**
This little hyena is covered thickly with white spots on a browny-red background. A pipe-bowl, with identical head, in Dunhill's collection of pipes, may have been made by the same man.

**8ab**    **Standing male figure. Dinka(?) tribe. Wood. l. 57 cm. Museum für Völkerkunde, Berlin.**

This elongated figure could be a text-book illustration of the typical pole-sculpture style. The features are crudely worked; holes for eyes and ears, the nose, lips and chin are chopped out from a projecting area on the face, and the teeth are shown by notches on the lips. This may be an ancestor figure. Its attribution to the Dinka is not certain, as one early authority states that the Dinka have no sculpture.

**9**    **Pipe-bowl in human form. Djour(?) tribe. Wood. h. 31.2 cm. British Museum, London.**

This pipe-bowl is carved in the shape of a standing woman, and, with the pipe-bowl illustrated in plate 10, are among the oldest pieces to come from this area, having been collected by Petherick before 1860. Their attribution to the Djour tribe is uncertain, as the Djour do not live near the Sobat river where these are said to have come from. In fact, a tamper from the same collection and area is typically Zande. These pipe-bowls, however, while showing some Congo influence, are hard to place with certainty.

**10**    **Pipe-bowl in human form. Djour(?) tribe. Wood. h. 31.3 cm. British Museum, London.**

As in plate 9, the head of this woman is hollowed out to form the pipe-bowl, and the stem comes out at the back of the neck, and was probably joined to a long hollow cane stem with a grass-filled gourd filter, as commonly used in this area for smoking hemp. The scarification on the body would seem to indicate Congo influence; the projecting navel is often regarded as a sign of beauty in African women. The ears, now somewhat damaged, had small lengths of stick stuck in all round the rims; this was a common form of adornment in this area.

**11**    **Standing figures. Bari tribe. Wood. h. (L–R) 55 cm, 46.5 cm. Museum für Völkerkunde, Vienna.**

These two ancestor figures are typical pole sculptures; another characteristic of this style is the pointed crown. The arms, joined to the sides, have a rather unusual lattice ornament. Eyes and nostrils are shown by burnt-in holes (the right-hand figure has studs in the eye-holes) and both have inserted teeth. They are probably by the same hand, and the one on the left may be female, the other male. It seems that these ancestor figures were kept inside the huts, where offerings were made to them, and that they were made by the Bari on the western banks of the Nile, and might be related to the sculpture of the Bongo and Zande tribes.

**12abc**    **Standing male figure. Bari tribe. Wood. h. 42 cm. Museum für Völkerkunde, Berlin.**

This figure seems to have been carved out of a bent piece of wood; certainly the pose is unusually stooping. While the head has the pointed crown characteristic of the pole style, the facial and bodily details are carved with unusual sensitivity and realism.

**13**    **Standing male figure. Bari/Dinka(?) tribes. Wood. h. 47 cm. Linden-Museum, Stuttgart.**

In treatment this ancestor figure resembles the one illustrated in plate 8, even to the lighter-coloured rectangular patch on the chest (the site of an old label?). Perhaps they come from the same source.

**14**    **Standing male figure. Bari tribe. Wood. h. 27 cm. Musée de l'Homme, Paris.**

The string round the neck and waist show how this ancestor figure would have been hung up inside the hut. Offerings were made to such ancestor figures, and their protection might be invoked for the living members of the family or tribal group.

**15**  **Standing male figure.  Bari tribe.  Wood.  h. 47 cm.  Musée de l'Homme, Paris.**
This male ancestor figure, in typical pole style, has a bulging forehead and realistic features that remind us of the figure illustrated in plate 12, though the carving, especially of the body, is less sensitive.

# SOUTH - WESTERN ETHIOPIA

**16**  **Tomb figures. Gato tribe. Wood. h. (L–R): 126 cm, 133 cm, 127 cm.  Museum für Völkerkunde, Frankfurt.**
These are typical examples of the tomb figures from southern Ethiopia, made of thick poles or tree-trunks with the top carved into a human head or head and shoulders. Often they are attributed to the related Konso tribe. These figures are made for brave and outstanding men; sometimes they have a phallic symbol attached to the front of the high crested head-dress. The vigorous carving of hair, beard and staring eyes, with these 'helmets' on top lend the figures an impressive dignity, even when, for ease of transport to Europe, they have been cut short just below the 'shoulders'; they can stand about 4 feet high when *in situ*, with more of the post underground, making the whole thing some 6 feet high.
These three figures, the central one wearing a phallic symbol, formed a single group of tomb figures, and were collected by the Frobenius expedition in 1950–2; they may then have been about 20–30 years old.

**17ab**  **Tomb figure.  Gato tribe.  Wood.      h. 120 cm. Linden-Museum, Stuttgart.**
This is another tomb figure, this time shown in profile and with a good bit of the lower part of the post, showing its trunk-like appearance, visible in the photograph.

*Central East Africa*

# THE INTERLACUSTRINE REGION AND THE EASTERN SHORES OF LAKE TANGANYIKA

**18**  **Mask.  Ziba tribe.  Wood.      h. 49 cm. Linden-Museum ,Stuttgart.**
This face mask has holes for eyes and mouth, the latter filled with animal teeth. Lines of white paint and a long black beard of colobus monkey fur heighten the effect of this mask. Masks of the type illustrated here and in plates 19 and 20 are said to be worn by a court jester.

**19**  **Mask.  Ziba tribe.  Wood.      h. 31 cm. Musée de l'Homme, Paris.**
This face mask, though unadorned by white paint or beard, is so similar in its treatment of face and toothed mouth as to make its attribution to the same tribe as plates 18 and 20 a certainty.

**20ab**  **Mask.  Ziba tribe.  Wood.      h. 23.5 cm. Linden-Museum, Stuttgart.**
This face mask has a large beard of colobus monkey fur, and eyebrows of similar material. A line of white paint runs round the face and eye-holes, across the cheek-bones and down the forehead and strongly aquiline nose. The mouth has inset teeth.

**21**  **Bull.  Karagwe tribe.  Iron.      h. 20 cm. Linden-Museum, Stuttgart.**
This is a beautifully formalized linear portrayal of a bull, in wrought iron, with the curve of the horns used as the basic feature for identifying the subject. As these figures (plates 21–4) were discovered by the Stanley expedition in 1876, we can safely rule out the idea

of European influence. Given the intractable material, these figures are correspondingly no more simplified than those made of clay (for example, plates 143–4, 146). No other iron sculpture is known in East Africa, but it occurs in Nigeria and Dahomey. These pieces (plates 21–4) came from the palace of Chief Rumanika of Karagwe; their exact purpose is not known.

**22     Bull.   Karagwe tribe.   Iron.       h. 31 cm. Linden-Museum, Stuttgart.**
The horns of this bull are more similar in appearance to those of East African cattle than those of the bull in plate 21, but cattle with deformed horns were often valued.

**23     Antelope.   Karagwe tribe.   Iron.       h. 36.5 cm. Linden-Museum, Stuttgart.**
This represents a long-horned humped antelope. The realistic treatment of the udder is in contrast to the absence of genitalia on the two bulls.

**24     Bird.   Karagwe tribe.   Copper.       h. 34 cm. Linden-Museum, Stuttgart.**
This stylized figure of a bird was made of sheet copper, again an unusual medium for an African craftsman, and which makes us wonder if a foreign artist at the court of Chief Rumanika was responsible for these pieces, of which this and the foregoing are the most striking.

**25     Bird.   Urundi.   Wood.       h. 12 cm. Linden-Museum, Stuttgart.**
This stylized figure, with its angular form, is a typically East African piece. Sculpture is normally absent in Ruanda and Urundi except as an introduction from the Congo.

**26     *Mkissi* figure.   Ha tribe.   Wood.     h. 30 cm. Museum für Völkerkunde, Berlin.**
Standing figure wrapped in a cotton garment coloured red, black and white. The simple treatment of the face, with its hooded eyes, gives it an enigmatic expression.

**27ab    Standing male figure.   Jiji tribe.   Wood.    h. 28 cm. Linden-Museum, Stuttgart.**
The treatment of the almond-shaped eyes, and the bodily scarification of this figure indicate some influence from the Congo. This is a robust carving, with its short sturdy legs and gun grasped firmly in the right hand. The loin-cloth is made of coarse twill.

**28     Standing figures.   Jiji tribe.   Wood.     h. 33.5 cm. Linden-Museum, Stuttgart.**
Although very similar to the preceding figure, this carving is probably by another hand. Here again the treatment of the eyes and face, and the bodily scarification, point to influence from the Congo.

**29ab    Standing female figure. Bende tribe. Wood. h. 67 cm. Museum für Völkerkunde, Berlin.**
Little is known of the Bende or their carving apart from this and the two other figures found with it. There is obvious affinity to Luba carving, but it does not fit in with any known Luba sub-style. If this piece in fact came from 'Urua' (the Swahili name for Luba country in the Congo) it cannot be included as a piece of genuine East African sculpture, though it serves well to illustrate the transmission of artistic styles from the Congo area.

**30     Antelope.   Fipa tribe.   Wood.       h. 27 cm. Linden-Museum, Stuttgart.**
This carving shows Congo influence in the treatment of the eyes. The head is well and realistically carved, but the anatomy of the legs is rather curious.

**31     Crocodile.   Fipa tribe.   Wood.       l. 48 cm. Linden-Museum, Stuttgart.**
Though superficially like a headrest or stool in form, the serrated ridge along the back of this figure would make it rather uncomfortable for this purpose.

# CENTRAL TANZANIA

**32**     **Standing male figure. Sukuma, Zinka or Sanaki tribes. Wood. h. 93 cm. Linden-Museum, Stuttgart.**

This, like so many of the sculptures from the Lakes Region of East Africa, shows some Congo influence in its stance and the treatment of its face. But as usual, it is hard to pinpoint the area or tribe from which this influence came.

**33**     **Standing female figures. Kerewe tribe. Wood. h. (L–R) 39 cm, 36 cm. Linden-Museum, Stuttgart.**

These, despite their attribution, are not very similar to the figure in Berlin illustrated by Fagg (1964, Pl. 94), or the figure in the British Museum which he thinks may be by a Kerewe carver, despite its attribution to the Ganda tribe. The Berlin figure, which is said to be an ancestor figure of a chief, and is 109.5 cm. high, must fall into a different category to these female figures, which look more recent, and were probably carved for a different purpose. The hair is shown by strings of beads or plant fibres.

**34**     **Standing female figure. Sukuma tribe. Wood. h. 50 cm. Linden-Museum, Stuttgart.**

This carving is not very far removed from the pole-style, and is in many ways similar to the two Kerewe figures in plate 33. The facial features are more clearly defined, and more attention is paid to bodily detail, but the treatment and attachment of the hair is strikingly alike, as also the overall appearance of the figure.

**35**     **Standing female figure. Sukuma tribe. Baked clay. h. 23.5 cm. Museum für Völkerkunde, Berlin.**

This representation of a woman is unlikely to be a child's toy as these appear to be mostly animals; here, however, the pronounced buttocks and *mons Veneris* would make this figure eminently suitable for puberty initiation ceremonies, or spirit dances, as described by Baumann.

**36**     **Carved pipe-stem. Nyamwezi tribe. Composite. h. 36 cm. Museum für Völkerkunde, Berlin.**

Clay pipe-bowl with a separately-made carved wooden stem and metal mouth-piece. The stem is ornamented with a male figure standing clear and modelled in the round: the face is typically 'East African' but the carved scarification marks are suggestive of Congo influence. The eyes are made with trade beads.

**37ab**     **Chief's throne. Nyamwezi tribe. Wood. h. 107 cm. Museum für Völkerkunde, Berlin.**

This throne is essentially a tripod stool in a form quite normal for this area, but which has had a high back added to it. This high back has a human figure carved in relief behind it, with projecting head and hands. This one was collected in 1898 from the palace of the Sultaness at Buruku.

**38**     **Horn. Zambia or Tanzania. Horn. l. 18 cm. Collection of René Vander Straete, Brussels.**

The size of this horn indicates that it was a powder-flask or snuff-bottle, with a separate wooden base, fitted into the wider end. It is hard to place this piece with any certainty, but somewhere around the south end of Lake Tanganyika seems possible. The hole, through which the gun-powder or snuff was shaken out, is on the 'chest' of the human figure which has been carved in relief on the horn.

**39ab**  **Horn. Zambia or Tanzania. Horn. l. 13 cm. Collection of René Vander Straete, Brussels.**

This horn is also a powder-horn or snuff-bottle, with a separate wooden base fitted. It is carved in relief to represent a woman with a child on her back; the child's pose recalls that of the figure on the back of the Nyamwezi throne. The scarification on the woman's face suggests some Congo influence. The opening is in the crown of the woman's head, and would have had a small stopper of wood or vegetable fibre.

**40abc**  **Standing female figures. Hehe tribe. Wood. h. 27 cm. Museum für Völkerkunde, Hamburg.**

This carving is very similar in treatment to the Jiji carvings in plates 27 and 28, and doubtless owes some of this likeness to the same influence from the Congo. The almond-shaped eyes recur in the Congo-influenced carvings of our area down to Barotseland in Zambia, where Lozi art is subject to Lunda influence (compare plate 122).

**41**  **Animal figures. Hehe tribe. Clay. l. (L–R): 12 cm, 12 cm. Linden-Museum, Stuttgart.**

These are probably made as children's toys. Despite their simplicity, they manage to catch the salient features of the bull (left) and the dog (right).

**42**  **Staffs. Hehe tribe. Wood. h. (L–R): 144 cm, 90 cm, 102 cm, 101 cm. Linden-Museum, Stuttgart.**

These staffs, surmounted with human heads, are more typically 'East African' than the female figure in plate 40. Characteristic features are the use of pokerwork decoration and trade-beads for eyes. The hair on the three heads to the right is carved like a raised disc reminiscent of the headrings in Ngoni carvings further to the south. They are most commonly used by village elders as a mark of dignity.

**43**  **Mask. Iraku tribe. Composite.          w. 16 cm. Linden-Museum, Stuttgart.**

Face mask made of animal skin with two ostrich feathers on top. The beadwork decoration on the forehead was made separately, in the same way as women's aprons or breast ornaments, and applied as one piece, while the beads surrounding the eye and mouth holes were threaded on one long thread and couched onto the mask.

# NORTH-EASTERN BANTU

**44**  *Nungu* **figure. Chaga tribe. Clay.          l. 20.2 cm. Néprajzi Museum, Budapest.**

These *nungu* figures (plates 44–7) were magical, and used to search out criminals. They are highly stylized, and beyond the information that the circular holes are the mouth and the vagina, it is hard to see what the different parts of this figure represent, though the parallel rows of six knobs could be arms, breasts and legs (compare plate 46).

**45**  *Nungu* **figure. Chaga tribe. Clay.          h. 9.7 cm. Néprajzi Museum, Budapest.**

This figure resembles some sort of animal, with an ill-defined round head at the top, four small knobs at the sides which might be legs, and a pointed extremity which might be a tail.

**46**  *Nungu* **figure. Chaga tribe. Clay.          h. 17.3 cm. Néprajzi Museum, Budapest.**

This has a recognizably human shape, with the head and face more carefully depicted than in plates 44–5, projections for arms, breasts and legs, and female genitalia.

**47**  *Nungu* **figure. Chaga tribe. Clay.          h. 14.5 cm. Néprajzi Museum, Budapest.**

This, though more stylized than plate 46, is still recognizably human, with the head separated from the body by a groove, holes for the facial features, and foot-like projections near the base, which seems to have a vaginal hole.

**48    Sitting figures. Kikuyu tribe. Clay. h. (L–R): 18 cm, 18 cm. British Museum, London.**
These roughly modelled clay figures show a man on the left, a woman on the right. Both are seated, and have stumpy arms and legs, with bits of grass-stem for teeth and ear ornaments. These figures were made and used during harvest-time dances held every two years.

**49    Sitting male figure.  Kahe tribe.  Clay.  h. 16.1 cm. Náprstek Museum, Prague.**
This shows a sitting man, with his knees drawn up, and the right arm bent, with the elbow resting on the right knee. The facial features are modelled with more care than is usual in this type of figure, and the pose is flexible. According to the collector, this figure was used for religious cults. There is a bit of coloured string round its neck.

**50    Standing figures. Arusha tribe. Clay. h. (L–R): 15.5 cm, 14 cm. Linden-Museum, Stuttgart.**
These figures are modelled as a pair, standing on stumpy legs, and with the head, arms and body crudely finished. The one on the left is male, the other female. As the Arusha, like the Kikuyu, are an agricultural tribe, these figures could, like the Kikuyu ones (plate 48), have been used during harvest ceremonies, or alternatively, during initiation rites.

**51    Sitting male figure.  Pare tribe.  Clay.  h. 26.1 cm. Náprstek Museum, Prague.**
This seated figure is roughly shaped, with a folded leaf for loin-cloth. The face is expressively modelled. Such figures might be placed in the yard of the hut to drive away thieves and enemies.

**52    Bottle-stopper.  Kahe tribe.  Wood.    l. 32.5 cm. Náprstek Museum, Prague.**
This stopper, with a roughly carved human head at one end, would have been used to close gourds containing magic symbols. Similar stoppers occur among the Pare tribe.

**53    Bull.  Chaga tribe.  Wood.            l. 51 cm. Néprajzi Museum, Budapest.**
This, though not a 'tourist piece' in the true sense of the word, is not a piece of native African art either. It appears that this and other figures were collected in 1902–3 and that they were carved by a talented wood-carver who had previously made only bowls, stools, etc. and who made these pieces at the collector's suggestion. This little bull shows how the carver used the shape and grain of the wood to suggest the pose.

**54    Standing female figure. Chaga tribe. Wood. h. 42.5 cm. Néprajzi Museum, Budapest.**
This figure, ornamented with strings of beadwork, with metal armlet and earrings, and with rattle anklets, is carved by the same man who did plates 53 and 55. While not un-'East African', these are not pieces of indigenous art, but rather a case of culture contact affecting an individual carver's talent.

**55    Figure of a monk. Chaga tribe. Wood. h. 54 cm. Néprajzi Museum, Budapest.**
The monk's body, clothed in a cassock, is extremely simplified, and the treatment of the face, which is similar to that of the *nungu* clay figures (plates 44–7), is explained by Vajda's statement that both the *nungu* figures and these figures of missionaries, monks and nuns are endowed with supernatural powers or represent people with supernatural powers.

**56    Standing female figure. Shambala tribe. Wood.    h. 38.5 cm. Linden-Museum, Stuttgart.**

The Shambala are one of the few East African tribes from whom traditional carvings have been collected. This vigorously stylized carving may perhaps represent an ancestor or cult figure.

**57    Bottle-stopper. Shambala tribe. Wood. Size of head: 5.5 cm. Linden-Museum, Stuttgart.**

This stopper for gourd bottles probably served a supernatural purpose to keep magical symbols within its container. The head with its bulging forehead, broad nose and wide mouth is most attractively stylized, and the curve of the outstretched arms bridges the gap between the head and the stopper itself.

**58    Stool.   Shambala tribe.   Wood.         l. 62.5 cm. Linden-Museum, Stuttgart.**

This stool is described as being carved in the shape of a hyena, which is possible, but not obvious. The whole animal is nicely stylized, the line of the back and the solid, slightly bent legs expressing its supporting function as a stool.

**59    Staff. Zaramo tribe. Wood. h. (of carving) 27 cm. Museum für Völkerkunde, Berlin.**

This staff, ending in a human torso, is one of a kind called *tambiko* and used as ordinary men's staffs which can also help in curing sick children; the sick child must hold his father's staff and believe that its magical properties will cure him.

**60    *Mwana kiti* doll.   Zaramo tribe.   Wood.        h. 18 cm. Museum für Völkerkunde, Hamburg.**

This highly stylized doll is formed by the combination of geometrical shapes to approximate to human form, enhanced here by a crest of fibre hair decorated with berries, and some incised ornamentation round the 'body'. These dolls were carried by maidens and women until the birth of the first child, a practice which occurs among other tribes of Africa, such as the Ashanti of Ghana, and the Zulu and Sotho of South Africa.

**61    *Mwana kiti* doll. Zaramo tribe. Wood. h. 14 cm. Museum für Völkerkunde, Berlin.**

This figure, though basically as cubistic as that in plate 60, is embellished by breasts and a prominent navel or umbilical hernia, commonly admired in Africa as a sign of beauty. There is a long-many-stranded necklace of trade beads. Perhaps this, like the *akua ba* dolls of Ghana, was to 'tell the woman's body to bear a baby as beautiful as this doll'.

**62    *Mwana kiti* doll. Doei tribe. Wood. h. 6.5 cm. Museum für Völkerkunde, Vienna.**

This figure, though highly stylized, is so much more naturalistic than the preceding two that we can see the steps by which the dolls have been formalized into cubist constructions. Here the face and head, though reduced to geometric planes, are quite recognizable as such, and we could infer that the favoured style of hairdressing was in the form of two ridges or crests from front to back.

**63    Standing male figure. Bondei tribe. Wood. h. 35 cm. Horniman Museum, London.**

This little carving would appear to represent a man wearing coastal Arab dress—a turban with part hanging down at the back, a tunic and trousers. The face is realistically carved.

# SOUTHERN TANZANIA

**64ab**    **Mask. Ngindo tribe. Wood.    h. 25 cm. Museum für Völkerkunde, Frankfurt.**
Face mask, stained a dark colour, with two semicircular areas of incised decoration showing the natural colour of the wood.

**65ab**    **Stool. Ngindo tribe. Wood. l. 53 cm. Collection of Kegel, Kegel & Konietzko, Hamburg.**
This zoomorphic stool is heavily ornamented with incised lattice decoration. On the back the decoration is arranged within a circle and includes two stylized human figures apparently standing on the backs of animals.

**66ab**    *Mbavala* **mask. Mwera tribe. Wood. l. 45 cm. Museum für Völkerkunde, Berlin.**
This face mask obviously represents an antelope, though the long beak-like muzzle seems to suggest that the features of more than one species of animal have been combined, which is quite usual in African art. The holes round the circumference of the face were for attaching the costume, usually made of vegetable fibres such as sisal grass, or of cloths, which served to conceal the dancer's body and preserve his anonymity.

**67**    **Mask. Mwera tribe. Wood.    l. 60 cm. Museum für Völkerkunde, Berlin.**
This face mask has two long hare-like ears, and a human-looking face with eyelashes and a long beard, probably of monkey fur. There is a resemblance in style and treatment to some of the Makonde masks.

**68**    **Doll. Kissi tribe. Clay.    h. 20 cm. Museum für Völkerkunde, Berlin.**
The Kissi women, in addition to making pots which were sold over a wide area, made little clay figures like this one. This is highly stylized but is nevertheless recognizable as a female figure, with small head tilting backwards, short stumpy legs, and five protuberances on the front which can be identified as arms, breasts, and prominent umbilical hernia (a sign of beauty), and with impressed ornament on the sides and above and below the navel, which may represent bodily scarification.

*The Southern Part of East Africa*

# NORTHERN MOZAMBIQUE

**69ab**    **Mask. Northern Mozambique. Wood. h. 51 cm. Museum für Völkerkunde, Berlin.**
This is a helmet mask, unusual in that there are two supporting 'legs' at the back and front of the neck. A hole is visible at the side of the neck for attaching the costume. These helmet masks were commonly worn by small boys who were able to wear them right over their heads and see through the perforated eyeholes. The pale-coloured groove along the line of the jaw is where a strip of fur was attached to represent the beard.
While the style of this mask allows it to be attributed to Northern Mozambique, it is different to the great majority of the masks, face or helmet, that we can assign to the Makonde and related tribes.

**70**    **Mask. Northern Mozambique. Wood. h. 23 cm. Museum für Völkerkunde, Berlin.**
This face mask may be meant as a caricature. The long triangular nose is flanked by deep cheek grooves, there is one tiny ear, and the small slit of a mouth at the very bottom is fringed with strips of animal skin to represent a beard. Often these face masks were worn by grown men, who might dance on their own feet or on stilts, for entertainment at festival or the like. Stilt-dancing occurs chiefly in southern Tanzania.

**71**    **Mask. Northern Mozambique. Wood. h. 22 cm. Museum für Völkerkunde, Berlin.**
This face mask is typically Makonde, with the upper lip distorted by a *pelele*, or lip-plug, and the facial scarification shown in black beeswax, although the design does not conform to the correct pattern as illustrated by Weule. This, together with the treatment of the hair by attaching a piece of animal skin, may mean that this is an atypical and modern mask, or from a related tribe rather than from the Makonde themselves. On the other hand, the closely similar mask in plate 88 is attributed to the Makonde. Facial scarification is practised among the Makonde as among other tribes as a means of adornment as well as tribal identi-fication (different tribes having different designs), but opinion is divided about the lip-plugs. To the European and Arab eye, they are repulsive, and this may have given rise to the explanation that they were worn by the women to make the slave-traders leave them alone, and that this custom has continued long after it was necessary. Another theory is that lip-plugs were worn as amulets to protect one of the eight openings of the body. Yet another theory and a likely one, is that they were worn as ornaments; certainly the plugs may be embellished with metal spikes or inset glass beads. Men as well as women used to wear them, but now only the women do so.

**72ab**    **Mask. Northern Mozambique. Wood. h. 26 cm. Museum für Völkerkunde, Berlin.**
There is a slight similarity in the treatment of eyes and nose between this mask and the one in plate 69, but certainly not enough to attribute them to the same tribe, just to the same general area. The parted lips show filed upper teeth, which used to be a feature of the Makonde, and a tuft of animal hair is attached by a lump of beeswax. The incised lines on the face are a schematic rendering of scarification.

**73**    **Head. Northern Mozambique. Wood. h. 12 cm. Collection of M. Gilbert Perier, Brussels (formerly Frits den Berghe collection).**
Head with the lip-plug and filed teeth typical of the Makonde and related tribes. The scari-fication is shown by notches on cheeks and forehead, and the narrow eyes are inset with glass for greater realism. Separately-carved heads are rare in East Africa art, and occur only under European influence. It is probable that this head is part of a complete figure, but without the opportunity to examine the original, it is hard to express a firm opinion.

**74**    **Mask. Northern Mozambique. Wood. h. 30 cm. Linden-Museum, Stuttgart.**
This helmet mask shows many Makonde characteristics: facial scarification shown by engraved lines, filed teeth, a 'cut' in the hair-line, and narrow segment-shaped eyes with heavy upper eyelids. The costume was tied on round the neck and secured by string through the holes on each side.

**75**    **Mask.  Yao tribe.  Wood.                        h. 20 cm. Linden-Museum, Stuttgart.**
This helmet mask of a man wearing a white cap shows a degree of realism bordering on caricature. The extended line of the face, similar to that of the *Gelede* helmet masks of the Yoruba tribe, Southern Nigeria, is an example of 'corrected perspective'; the mask is worn on the top of the head but tilted slightly forwards so that the dancer can see out through the mouth; when worn in that way, the facial proportions seem all right. The hooded eyes, swollen upper lip, filed teeth, and treatment of the hair, are all typical of the related Southern Makonde (often called Mawia by other tribes as a derogatory term similar to Kaffir) of Northern Mozambique. A strip of animal skin for the beard must have been attached to the chin. The hair is realistically rendered by small amounts of human negro hair being pushed into small incisions in the scalp and additionally stuck down with beeswax.

**76**    **Mask. Makonde tribe. Wood. w. 34 cm. Museum für Völkerkunde, Hamburg.**
This face mask combines animal and human features. Nose and lip-plugged mouth are stylized and simply treated; eyebrows and eyelashes are outlined in beeswax, while the large ears

are those of an animal. This is the type of mask used to inspire terror in initiation ceremony dances.

**77ab**  **Standing female figure. Makonde tribe. Wood. h. 56.5cm. Museum für Völkerkunde, Berlin.**
This carving of a woman, with three toes and three fingers on feet and hands, may well be a cult-figure of a matriarch-founder of the tribe, such as Weule describes, and was collected by Stuhlmann in Mikindani in 1895. She has metal earrings, a lip-plug, and human hair stuck on with beeswax. The pose recalls that of the dancing women (plates 78–9).

**78**  **Dancing female figure. Makonde tribe. Wood. h. 74 cm. Linden-Museum, Stuttgart.**
This is the best of several Makonde figures of dancing women; movement is conveyed by the slightly flexed knees and the raised arms bent at the elbows. Naturalism is beautifully stylized and executed. The Makonde characteristics of lip-plug and human hair stuck on with beeswax are present, even though the piece is in a style totally different to that of the masks, unlike the figure in plate 80.

**79**  **Dancing female figure. Makonde tribe. Wood. h. 74 cm. Museum für Völkerkunde, Berlin.**
This carving of a dancing woman closely resembles that in plate 82, and may have been by the same hand. The eyes are more clearly seen to have been separately made in a lighter material to achieve realism. This figure has a bead necklace and ear-plugs which latter must have been present in the one in plate 78, judging by the holes in the ears.

**80**  **Standing male figure. Makonde tribe. Wood. h. 41.5 cm. Museum für Völkerkunde, Hamburg.**
This carving is probably a fairly modern piece. The face shows characteristics of the helmet masks, such as the shape of the (sightless) eyes, the angle of the profile and the fullness of the upper lip which persists in carvings even when there is no lip-plug to induce it. The bodily scarification is done in pokerwork, and the hair is stained black. Part of the lower lip has broken away, which, in the photograph, makes it look like a white beard.

**81**  **Standing female figure. Makonde tribe. Wood. h. 75 cm. Linden-Museum, Stuttgart.**
This seems to be a fairly modern and rather crude carving of an ancestor figure, rather than a more sophisticated work made for sale to Europeans. The use of applied beeswax to represent scarification, the human hair on its head, and the lip-plug are all characteristic of the Makonde group of tribes.

**82ab**  **Standing female figure. Mozambique(?). Wood.**      **h. 72.5 cm. Collection of M. and Mme. W. Mestach, Brussels.**
This carving, though ascribed to the Makonde, is far from what one might expect from that tribe, and one may wonder if it does not come from further south, or even from West Africa. The hair is made of lengths of string stuck onto the scalp, and there are a girdle and earrings of trade beads.

**83**  **Standing female figure. Northern Mozambique. Wood. h. 73.5 cm. Museum für Völkerkunde, Hamburg.**
This carving, ascribed to the Makonde, might be more safely attributed to Northern Mozambique, as in style it does not fit in with known Makonde carvings, while the treatment of eyes and mouth is not unlike that of the masks illustrated in plates 69 and 72. The nose however is strongly aquiline.

**84**     **Standing female figure. Makonde tribe. Wood. h. 59 cm. Museum für Völkerkunde, Hamburg.**

This may have been intended as another figure of a dancing woman since, even though the arms are only slightly bent, the whole pose suggests dance movement. The woman's eyes are made of beads, short strings of beads form earrings, and she has a large lip-plug.

**85**     **Woman with child. Makonde tribe. Wood. h. 73.5 cm. Museum für Völkerkunde, Hamburg.**

This shows a standing woman, wearing a lip-plug, and carrying a child on her shoulders. The faces of both woman and child show scarification marks, though scarification is not normally begun until initiation at puberty, when no child would be carried by its mother any longer.

**86**     **Mask. Makonde tribe. Wood. h. 19 cm. Museum für Völkerkunde, Hamburg.**

The large lip-plug is the dominant feature of this face mask. The hair is human hair stuck on with beeswax, the mask is covered with thick reddish paint except for the lip-plug which is coloured white.

**87**     **Mask. Makonde tribe. Wood. h. 21 cm. Museum für Völkerkunde, Hamburg.**

In this face mask, the line of eyebrows and nose serve well to balance the upper lip with its prominent plug. The small square eyes have hair eyelashes stuck on with beeswax, of which there are a few ornamental blobs as well as a strip across the forehead with hatching, presumably to indicate scarification. The small square ears have holes for ear ornaments, apparently in the form of knotted strips of cotton.

**88**     **Mask. Makonde tribe. Wood.          h. 18 cm. Linden-Museum, Stuttgart.**

This face mask is so similar to that illustrated in plate 71 that we may wonder if the same man carved both. The face is patterned with beeswax to represent scarification, and there is a lip-plug.

**89**     **Mask. Makonde tribe. Wood.          h. 22 cm. Museum für Völkerkunde, Berlin.**

The face mask, while it has the typical Makonde lip-plug, is different in its rendering of facial scarification. Normally, the beeswax shows a more or less faithful rendering of tribal markings, but the three rosettes on the forehead and the toothed circle enclosing the nose and mouth seem to be more decorative in intention. The hair and eyelashes are made from human hair; a double row of white beads edges the hairline, and similar beads make multiple earrings threaded through the rims of the ears. The holes for attaching the costume are plainly visible round the lower edge of the mask.

**90**     **Mask. Makonde tribe. Wood.          h. 16 cm. Linden-Museum, Stuttgart.**

This face mask shows a man with twisted nose and lopsided mouth and face, obviously indicating partial facial paralysis. Masks illustrating facial deformity such as paralysis, or gangosa (yaws) (in which the nose is eaten away, as in syphilis) occur among the Ibibio tribe of south-east Nigeria and elsewhere. Animal hair is stuck into a slit in the chin to represent a beard.

**91**     **Body mask. Makonde tribe. Wood.          h. 45 cm. Linden-Museum, Stuttgart.**

Body masks such as this were worn by dancers representing women in dances where a mime of sexual intercourse took place. The pointed breasts with long nipples, prominent navel and extensive scarification were all signs of beauty in a woman.

**92**     **Masks. Makonde tribe. Wood. h. (L–R) 8 cm, 9 cm. Linden-Museum, Stuttgart.**

This pair of masks (female on the left, male on the right), which were collected before 1905 and should therefore be traditional, appear to be miniature face masks. There are holes for attaching the costume, but there are no eye or mouth holes, so the dancers would have had to look through a hole in the costume. They may have been used in dances miming sexual intercourse.

The eyes seem to be made of beeswax, the female mask has two 'beauty spots', of the same material of which one may be a nose plug, and the male mask has a sisal-fibre beard stuck on with beeswax.

**93    Mask.   Makonde tribe.   Wood.         h. 22 cm. Museum für Völkerkunde, Vienna.**
This face mask is in a style quite different to any of those illustrated so far, and it is, in fact, with its pale face and long eyes, reminiscent of masks from Gaboon. The mouth is slightly open, showing pointed teeth, and the ears are set high, both Makonde characteristics.

**94    Mask. Makonde tribe. Wood. h. 22.5 cm. Museum für Völkerkunde, Hamburg.**
This face mask is again in a style different to that of the previously illustrated Makonde masks, and has a very brooding expression, partly created by the long nose, sheathed in applied metal. The partly open mouth has a beeswax moustache to which hair may have been attached, and the long eyeholes have wide borders.

**95    Mask.   Makonde tribe.   Wood.      h. 22 cm. Museum für Völkerkunde, Hamburg.**
This face mask, naturalistically carved, shows a strength and sensitivity of modelling akin to that shown in the dancing women in plates 78–9. The shaping of the upper lip and eyelids, and the high set of the square ears are characteristically Makonde.

**96    Mask.   Makonde tribe.   Wood.         h. 19 cm. Linden-Museum, Stuttgart.**
This face mask is a nice combination of interplaying curves, even if the total effect is somewhat obscured by the beard of animal hair stuck on with beeswax. The face is a pure oval, with other ovals or parts of ovals in the eye hollows, the ears, and the forehead ornament. There are traces of beeswax scarification, and the eyelashes are stuck on with beeswax. The eyes and small mouth are pierced.

**97    Mask.   Makonde tribe.   Wood.         h. 22 cm. Linden-Museum, Stuttgart.**
This face mask is carved in similar style to the preceding one. The eye hollows are filled in with balls of beeswax into which eyelashes are stuck; eyeholes are pierced through beeswax and wood. The small mouth is rimmed with beeswax, which is also used to attach the hair and beard, made of goat's or similar wool. Beeswax is also used to stick on coils of white tradebeads. This is considered to be one of the most beautiful of the Makonde face masks.

**98abc   Mask.   Makonde tribe.   Wood.         h. 27.5 cm. British Museum, London.**
This is a good example of the Makonde helmet mask, worn by small boys and covering the head. Unlike the face masks, the eyes are unpierced; the dancer looks through the mouth instead and the costume is tied on round the flaring neck. Scarification is particularly clearly outlined in beeswax; the hair is human, attached with beeswax and by being pushed into small cuts in the scalp. The swollen upper lip, pointed lower lip, filed teeth and hooded eyes are also typical of this style of mask.

**99    Mask.   Makonde tribe.   Wood.         h. 48 cm. Linden-Museum, Stuttgart.**
This is one of the face masks described as being of the devil, to cause terror during initiation ceremony dances. It has horns and a long beard made of sisal fibre, with a human face.

**100    Mask.   Makonde tribe.   Wood.         h. 75 cm. Linden-Museum, Stuttgart.**
This face mask combines animal and human features, and in a way is similar to the mask illustrated in plate 67, from the Mwera tribe in southern Tanzania. This mask, too, has long

hare-like ears and a beard, and also scarification shown by inlaid strips of white metal, and is the sort of mask used in initiation ceremony dances.

**101**      **Mask. Makonde tribe. Wood. h. 51 cm. Museum für Völkerkunde, Hamburg.**
This mask is unusual in that the facial scarification is shown by dark paint on a lighter surface. The hair, eyes and eyelashes are also painted, while the beard seems to be of raffia or similar fibre. A lip-plug distorts the upper lip, showing that they were not worn exclusively by women. It looks as if the dancer saw through a hole in the upper lip rather than through eyes or mouth.

**102**      **Mask. Yao tribe. Wood.      h. 26 cm. Museum für Völkerkunde, Hamburg.**
This helmet mask, while attributed to the Yao tribe shows many Makonde characteristics such as the use of human hair, hooded eyes, small nose and lip-plug. The lip-plug here has led to the upper lip being shown in unusually distorted form, to the extent of caricature.

**103**      **Toy bull. Makonde tribe. Clay.      h. 8 cm. Museum für Völkerkunde, Berlin.**
This stylized model of a bull, made as a toy, as in many other East and South African tribes, may be said to show the Makonde tendency to caricature in the greatly exaggerated hump.

**104**      **Mask. Makonde tribe. Wood. h. 28 cm. Museum für Völkerkunde, Hamburg.**
This helmet mask, when seen beside more traditionally-carved masks, shows how the standards of craftsmanship can decline. The carving is not particularly well done, little care seems to have been taken to finish or polish the surface of the wood, and the scarification is roughly done in pokerwork. It compares unfavourably with the mask illustrated in plate 98, which is more traditional. If carved for use and not for sale, the dancer presumably looked through a gap in the costume, as the mask itself is unperforated.

**105**      **Staff. Makonde tribe. Wood. h. 75.5 cm. Museum für Völkerkunde, Hamburg.**
This staff, adorned with the carved figure of a woman, is quite a good example of modern Makonde work. The head is carved in a manner similar to that of the helmet masks, though the scarification is shown by areas of raised carved surfaces stained a darker colour.

**106**      **Kneeling female figure. Mawia tribe. Wood. h. 49 cm. Náprstek Museum, Prague.**
This is a recent carving, made for sale to Europeans. The head resembles the helmet masks, and pokerwork is used to render scarification on face and abdomen, and to colour the hair and skirt.
The Mawia should more properly be called the southern Makonde; they are the Makonde living in Mozambique, south of the Rovuma river on the Tanzania-Mozambique border, and their masks are normally helmet masks. The Makonde on the north of the Rovuma, in Tanzania, tend to carve face masks.

# THE TERRITORY TO THE WEST AND SOUTH OF LAKE NYASA

**107**      **Standing female figure. Bemba tribe. Wood. h. 53.4 cm. Horniman Museum, London.**
This carving is a good example of Congo-influenced East African work. The figure itself is carved without elaboration, with long cylindrical body and limbs, and small round head; but the scarification of face and chest, and the incised ovals of eyes and mouth show Congo influence.

**108**  **Mask.  Eastern Zambia.  Composite.**  **h. 31 cm. Musée de l'Homme, Paris.**

This face mask is made of coarse barkcloth on a stick frame, with hair and beard of animal skin. The 'wen' on the forehead, the eyebrow ridge and nose are apparently applied, while the eyes and mouth are made by slitting the barkcloth and raising the surface. The horizontal painted lines may indicate that this mask was used in initiation ceremonies. Barkcloth masks occur in Angola and the southern Congo as well as Zambia. Somewhat similar masks from the Lovale tribe may be worn with a closefitting polychrome net garment, with fibre kilt and leglets, or with a large conical body mask of painted barkcloth on a stick foundation.

**109**  **Mask.  Mambwe tribe.  Wood.**  **h. 29 cm. Horniman Museum, London.**

This face mask shows a certain likeness to those carved by the Ziba tribe (plates 18–20). The face is reduced to its simplest essentials of form, with square holes for eyes and mouth, the teeth in the latter being from an antelope or similar ruminant.

**110**  **Standing figure. Blantyre region of Malawi. Wood. h. 54.8 cm. British Museum, London.**

The set of the legs in this carving is somewhat similar to that in the carving from the Bemba tribe (plate 107), but this figure is more crudely carved. The pose has a certain uncouth vigour, the face is realistically carved, the realism being heightened by the use of shell for the eyes and teeth, and animal skin for the hair. This carving seems to be by the same hand as that in plate 112, and the lack of breasts in this may indicate that it is not a female figure as stated by the British Museum, but an undeveloped girl or more probably a man, since the appearance of the genitalia suggests that the deep hole in the pubic region may have been for the attachment of a penis. In that case we would have a family group of man and woman with young child.

**111**  **Standing female figure. Blantyre region of Malawi. Wood. h. 76 cm. British Museum, London.**

This, though from the same area and collection as those illustrated in plates 110 and 112, is very different in treatment; one would say a different tribe. In form this is more of a pole-sculpture, the face is flattened in a manner suggesting a face mask, and human hair is used on head and pubis. The breasts and navel are outlined by incised circles; they and the hands are in a lighter colour than the rest of the body, which is ochre red. There is a nose-plug of the type worn by Makua and Lomwe women.

**112ab**  **Standing woman with child. Blantyre region of Malawi. Wood. h. 65 cm. British Museum, London.**

This seems to be carved by the same hand as the one in plate 110. The stance is very similar, also the treatment of faces and hair. Since it is hard to see how these pieces, carved before 1909, fit into the ethnography of the area, we may wonder if they were early mission carvings, or the produce of a talented carver who normally made utilitarian objects (compare the Chaga carvings in plates 53–5).

**113**  **Standing female figure. Lomwe tribe. Wood. h. 35 cm. Museum für Völkerkunde, Berlin.**

This and the figure in plate 114 are two pieces collected in 1901 from the Anguru (a group of the Lomwe tribe) of Lake Chilwa. This little carving has an appealingly stylized face with protruding wedge-shaped lips, the upper lip having a bead for lip-plug. The hair is shown by a carved crest with human hair attached, and scarification in the form of incised lines is shown on face, abdomen, sides and thighs. The tiny arms are in contrast to the large box-like feet. Both this and the next carving may have been cult figures, representing female tribal ancestors.

**114abc**   Standing female figure. Lomwe tribe. Wood. h. 40.3 cm. Museum für Völkerkunde, Berlin.

Although this was collected from the same tribe as the figure in plate 113, the two carvings are quite different in proportions of the body and treatment of the face. The woman is standing on a stool-shaped base; her body and face are covered with lines representing scarification, but in a manner suggesting that the carver's aim was more to cover the whole bodily surface than reproduce tribal scars. The treatment of the concave face is interestingly formalized.

**115ab**   Standing female figure. Maravi tribes. Wood. h. 56 cm. Museum für Völkerkunde, Berlin.

In its pose, with straddled legs, long cylindrical body and large feet, and scarification of face and body, this carving is reminiscent of pieces from the Bemba and Lomwe tribes, although showing plenty of differences as well. The technique of carving the zig-zag lines is one very typical of this area.

**116**   Mask.   Chemba tribe.   Wood.        h. 34 cm. Linden-Museum, Stuttgart.

This face mask is like some of the Makonde masks. Obviously this one has had horns or more likely long ears, now broken off, which, with the beard of animal skin, indicate that this mask was used in initiation ceremony dances. Beeswax has been used around the eyes and mouth to attach hair, on the scalp, and to represent scarification.

*South Africa*

# CENTRAL ZAMBEZI

**117**   Food dish.   Zambia.   Wood.        l. 45.1 cm. Musée d'ethnographie, Antwerp.

This food dish, while we have no precise documentation of its origin, is typical of those produced by the Lozi (often called Barotse) and related groups. The lids of these dishes were most commonly ornamented with carved ducks, but, fostered by the European market and tourists, a wider variety of animals now occur on these food dishes, and the separately-carved animals find a ready sale to tourists.

**118**   Food dish. Lozi tribe. Wood.   l. 48.5 cm. Musée Royale de l'Afrique Centrale, Tervuren.

This dish, with its perforated rim and legs, is unusual in form, whereas the figures of feeding birds, stylized into segments on a single leg, are quite typical.

**119**   Food dish.   Lozi tribe.   Wood.   l. 36 cm. Museum für Völkerkunde, Frankfurt.

In its oval shape, with the three stylized figures of swimming ducks on the lid, this is a classic example of the distinctive and attractive food dishes from this area, which are carved from a light wood, stained and polished black on the outside.

**120**   Stool.   Lozi tribe.   Wood.        h. 42 cm. Museum für Völkerkunde, Hamburg.

The circular seat of this stool is supported by two legs resting on the back of an antelope, itself standing on a circular base.

**121**   Food dish.   Lozi tribe.   Wood.        l. 40 cm. Museum für Völkerkunde, Frankfurt.

This is another classic example of the food dishes from this area, often labelled Barotse, or Barotse-land, and it shows how the basic duck theme can be varied.

**122ab**   Kneeling woman with dish. Lozi tribe. Wood. h. 56.5 cm. British Museum, London.

This was collected in Barotseland and is a good example of figure carving from that area.

The 'wings' coming out on each side of the face, the shape of the eyes and treatment of scarification indicate Lunda influence. The great Lunda empire spread its influence from Angola, where the Jokwe tribe have similar 'wings' on their carvings, the southern Congo and Zambia. A conus-shell disc and some metal rattle-beads are attached to one arm.

**123ab  Standing female figure. Lozi tribe(?). Horn. h. 6.6 cm. Collection of René Vander Straete, Brussels.**

Figure carvings in horn, such as this one, are unusual in African art. M. Vander Straete has two closely similar ones; illustrated here has facial scarifications identical to those on the female figure in plate 39, also in his collection. The attribution to one of the Rotse tribes is tentative only, but this carving must come from somewhere in the general region of eastern Zambia, or around the south end of lake Tanganyika. The realistic carving also of thighs and knees in this figure is in contrast to the rough treatment of the upper part.

**124  Mask.  Mbunda tribe.  Wood.       h. 32.5 cm. British Museum, London.**

This and similar face masks have been attributed to the Subia tribe of Zambia by von Sydow and others; however Dr. J. D. Clark, formerly director of the Rhodes-Livingstone Museum in Zambia, attributed this and a similar mask in the British Museum collections to the Mbunda tribe, saying that they were called *samahongo*, and were used in the *makishi* dances held every fortnight at Shesheke, the capital town. These masks, with deeply grooved foreheads, often bulging cheeks, and square or oval mouths open to show pointed teeth, are most distinctive, especially when worn surmounted by a high crest of feathers. This mask is more austere than some.

**125  Headrest.  Totela tribe.  Wood.       h. 12.2 cm. British Museum, London.**

The form of this headrest, as to its top and base, is typical of those produced by the Shona group of tribes, whereas the caryatid support is more akin to Congo work. The head, neck and shoulders are treated almost architecturally; the arms are just stumps, and the face is not elaborated. There is a girdle of coiled wire round the base.

# R H O D E S I A

**126  Pottery vessel.  Zezuru tribes.  Pottery.  h. 22 cm. Museum für Völkerkunde, Frankfurt.**

This pot, which comes from the Wedza region of Rhodesia, is characteristic of the Zezuru vessels, made with bichrome decoration and zoomorphic to greater or lesser degree. This one has two stumps for legs, and four necks on top. In other parts of Africa, pots with multiple necks, or anthropomorphic or zoomorphic features, are used for magical or ritual purposes, and this may be the case with this and the following two pots as well. The ware is red, with triangular zones burnished black.

**127  Pottery vessel.  Zezuru tribes.  Pottery.  h. 27 cm. Museum für Völkerkunde, Frankfurt.**

This, another pot from the Wedza region, is much more obviously zoomorphic than the previous one, since it has four legs and the neck comes out of the body in such a way as to suggest an animal's head. The arrangement of the black and red triangles enhances the zoomorphic effect.

**128  Pottery vessel.  Zezuru tribes.  Pottery.  h. 36 cm. Museum für Völkerkunde Hamburg.**

Here it is mainly the four little legs that give the zoomorphic effect, since the two necks come out symmetrically at each end of the body. Like the others, it is embellished with burnished black triangles on a red ground.

**129**  **Mask. Zezuru tribes. Wood.    h. 37 cm. Museum für Völkerkunde, Hamburg.**

This face mask is very similar to those produced by the Mbunda tribe (see plate 124), but this one is carved in a less vigorous manner, and there are two horns, similar to those of the duiker antelope, instead of a lateral ridge to which a large crest of feathers is attached.

## SOUTH-EAST AFRICA

**130**  **Standing figures. Nguni/Thonga tribes. Wood. h. (L–R) 94.6 cm, 94.6 cm. Rijksmuseum voor Volkenkunde, Leiden.**

Since we know in the case of the Ronga, one of the Thonga tribes, that there are no ancestor figures, despite a strong ancestor cult, it may be that none of these Nguni/Thonga figures are ancestor carvings, and in that case it is hard to say what they were carved for, unless in some response to European influence. Both are carved in the pole style, with features picked out in pokerwork. The man, on the right, has a *keshla* head-ring. When a man among these tribes (which include the Zulu) reaches a certain dignity and age, he is entitled to wear one of these head-rings, which is made by mixing black beeswax and gum in with the growing hair, and polishing the smooth ring thus formed.

**131**  **Standing female figure. Nguni/Thonga tribes. Wood. h. 59.3 cm. Rijksmuseum voor Volkenkunde, Leiden.**

This carving is unusual in that the body comes out of a single leg placed symmetrically in the centre. Otherwise it fits in well with the known series of Nguni/Thonga carvings.

**132**  **Standing figures. Thonga/Magwamba tribes. Wood. h. (L–R) 55 cm, 57 cm. British Museum, London.**

This is a pair of figures, female on the left, male (with head-ring) on the right, similar to those in plates 130 and 133–4. These were collected before 1893 and are to be reckoned as old carvings.

**133**  **Standing figures. Nguni/Thonga tribes. Wood. h. (L–R) 70 cm, 68.5 cm. Rijksmuseum voor Volkenkunde, Leiden.**

While carved as a pair, these figures show a striking difference in the carving of the arms. The man (on the left, wearing a head-ring) has short arms hanging straight down, with only a slight indication of the elbow-joint; while the woman (right) has long boneless arms which form a loop where the elbows ought to be.

**134**  **Standing figures. Nguni/Thonga tribes. Wood. h. (L–R) 60.5 cm, 59 cm. Rijksmuseum voor Volkenkunde, Leiden.**

This is another pair. The man, on the left, has a head-ring and beard, and wears a fringed loin cloth of animal skin, while the woman on the right has a piece of cloth round her hips.

**135**  **Standing female figure. Zulu tribe. Wood. h. 48 cm. Rijksmuseum voor Volkenkunde, Leiden.**

The similarity in style between Zulu figures such as this and following ones and the preceding Nguni/Thonga pieces is readily explained by the fact that the Zulu tribe is one of the Nguni/Thonga group. Unless precisely documented, it is usually hard to attribute a given carving to one Nguni tribe rather than another.

**136ab**  **Standing male figure. Zulu tribe. Wood. h. 57.5 cm. Rijksmuseum voor Volkenkunde, Leiden.**

This is a good example of a Zulu carving of somewhat more recent date than those illustrated in plates 130–135, which are all of the same lineage. These earlier pieces, usually before 1900 in date, are normally left in the pale natural colour of the wood, with features picked out in pokerwork, while later carvings are stained and polished black, and the carving is usually more sophisticated.

**137**     **Standing male figure. Zulu tribe. Wood. h. 52.5 cm. Rijksmuseum voor Volkenkunde, Leiden.**

This, to judge by the museum's numbering and also by its appearance, is almost certainly a male counterpart to the female figure illustrated in plate 135, and they are by the same carver. This male figure lacks a head-ring.

**138**     **Standing female figure. Zulu tribe. Wood. h. 20.5 cm. Museum für Völkerkunde, Vienna.**

The carver of this figure has made up for his lack of expertise in naturalistic carving by the great vigour of his rendering of arms, shoulders and legs. By contrast with these and the broad neckless head, the body is slim and almost weedy.

**139**     **Staffs. Zulu tribe. Wood. h. (L–R) 107 cm, 120 cm, 111 cm, 118 cm, 115 cm. Rijksmuseum voor Volkenkunde, Leiden.**

These five staffs, probably for village elders, are all surmounted by heads carved in the typical Nguni/Zulu style. All except the first on the left are shown with the *keshla* or head-ring (see caption to plate 130) and the central head shows graphically how it its attached to the growing hair on the head. The head on the far right is curious—'a face within a face', so to speak. The dark parts on all five heads are coloured by pokerwork.

**140**     **Headrests. Nguni/Zulu tribes. Wood. h. (L–R) 15 cm, 15.5 cm. Rijksmuseum voor Volkenkunde, Leiden.**

This is a pair of headrests, the one on the left representing a rhinoceros, that on the right, an elephant. Traditional Zulu headrests are not zoomorphic, and these are more likely to be from a Nguni/Thonga group further to the north than the Zulu proper. The functionally shaped upper parts of the headrests with the two lugs, is a feature showing Shona influence (compare plate 125). The dark parts of the carvings are coloured by pokerwork.

**141**     **Doll. Zulu tribe. Composite. h. 15 cm. Collection of René Vander Straete, Brussels.**

These clay dolls were made as children's toys and probably also as charms for young girls or childless women, to induce fertility or the birth of beautiful children. This little doll, modelled in clay, has the face visible, otherwise the whole surface is covered with strings of trade beads, the strings forming the 'skirt' ending in seeds.

**142**     **Doll. Zulu tribe. Composite. h. 17 cm. Collection of Joseph Vander Straete, Musée Ribaudi, Lasne, Brabant.**

This doll is bottle-shaped and the whole surface is covered with trade beads. At the very top two white beads represent eyes set in a dark face. Some of these dolls are in fact made with beer-bottles or cartridge-cases as a core.

## SOUTH AFRICA

**143**     **Bull. Sotho tribe. Clay.                h. 9.5 cm. Musée de l'Homme, Paris.**

This, and the bull illustrated in plate 145, are typical of the animals (most commonly cattle) modelled by children and used by them as toys. Bulls seem to be favourite animals among the Basuto; they and the Zulu made snuff-bottles in the form of realistically modelled small bulls in a technique akin to papier-mâché but using scrapings of animal-skin or entrails while fresh and sticky, modelled on to a clay core which is removed when the model is set.

**144**      **Animal figure.   Sotho tribe.   Clay.**      **h. 13 cm. British Museum, London.**

In its present state this creature is not immediately identifiable, but the catalogue drawing shows that it had horns (now broken off) and was probably a buffalo or gnu.

**145**      **Bull. Sotho tribe. Clay.**      **h. 8.5 cm. Musée de l'Homme, Paris.**

This is similar to the model shown in plate 143.

**146**      **Bull.   Sotho tribe.   Clay.**      **h. 8.7 cm. British Museum, London.**

This bull, which was collected before 1905, was fired in the hot ashes of the hearth, which gives it a glazed appearance.

**147**      **Doll.   Sotho tribe.   Composite.**      **h. 26 cm. British Museum, London.**

This doll has a clay head with sketched-in features and fibre hair, while the body is made of a beer-bottle covered in strings of trade beads. It is wrapped in a cloth kaross, or cloak, edged with beads, in imitation of the heavy karosses, made of a whole ox-skin, treated with red earth and edged with white or brass beads or buttons, which Sotho women used to wear before traders' blankets became universal.

**148**      **Doll. Ambo tribe. Composite. h. 36 cm. Collection of Kegel, Kegel & Konietzko, Hamburg.**

This doll could, like others illustrated earlier in this book, have served as a child's toy or as a charm to induce fertility or the birth of beautiful children. This doll consists of a wooden cylinder with a knob at each end, one of which is a simply-carved head, ornamented with bead earrings and with beads and buttons for hair. The 'body' is wrapped in strings of small beads, while strings of larger beads, with multiple short strings of small beads at the ends, represent arms with fingers, and legs with toes. There are girdles of hide, beads, and skin.

**149**      **Doll.   Sotho tribe.   Composite.**      **h. 25.5 cm. British Museum, London.**

This is an old doll, collected by a French missionary before 1870, yet quite similar to that illustrated in plate 147. It is a clay cone, of which only the head with beads for eyes and mouth is visible. Bead strings and fibre represent the hair, and there are earrings of brass wire. The leather kaross is elaborately worked and trimmed with white shirt-buttons, and ornamented with strings of beads and a fringe.

**150**      **Doll. Ambo tribe. Composite. h. 24 cm. Collection of Kegel, Kegel & Konietzko, Hamburg.**

This doll is similar in its dumb-bell shape to that in plate 148, and has its 'grip' covered with a continuous string of small beads. There is no carving of the 'head' however, and the double string of white beads could represent a necklet or a girdle. The hide band could serve as a loop for carrying or hanging.

**151**      **Headrest.   Ambo tribe.   Wood.**      **l. 47.5 cm. Musée de l'Homme, Paris.**

This headrest is carved in the form of a quadruped with large ears and a short tail, and what looks like a collar, so it might be a cow or bull. The body and head are covered with incised geometrical ornament; the triangular patches, painted red, are reminiscent of the decoration on Zezuru pottery (plates 126-8).

**152**      **Doll. Ambo tribe. Composite. h. 20 cm. Collection of Kegel, Kegel & Konietzko, Hamburg.**

This doll, though having the dumb-bell shape characteristic of this tribe, has its body hidden by strands of trade-beads giving the impression of a skirt; the head is covered with similar beads stuck on with clay or cattle dung, and the strings of smaller beads may represent necklets.

Adam, L. and Trimborn, H., 1958. *Lehrbuch der Völkerkunde*. Stuttgart.

Adams, A., 1902. *Lindi und sein Hinterland*. Berlin.

Barrett, W. E. H., 1911. 'Notes on the Customs and Beliefs of the Wa-Giriama, British East Africa' in *Journal of the Royal Anthropological Institute*, XLI, pp. 20–39.

Battiss, W. W., Franz, G. H., Grossert, J. W., Junod, H. P., 1958. *The Art of Africa*. Pietermaritzburg.

Baumann, H., Thurnwald, R., Westermann, D., 1940. *Völkerkunde von Afrika*. Essen.

Baumann, O., 1891. *Usambara und seine Nachbargebiete*. Berlin.

Baumann, O., 1894. *Durch Massailand zur Nilquelle*. Berlin.

Bent, J. T., 1892. *The Ruined Cities of Mashonaland*. London.

Blohm, W., 1933. *Die Nyamwezi: Gesellschaft und Weltbild*. Hamburg.

Bösch, F., 1930. *Les Banyamwezi*. Münster.

Caton-Thompson, G., 1931. *The Zimbabwe Culture: Ruins and Reactions*. Oxford.

Christol, F., 1911. *L'art dans l'Afrique australe*.

Clark, J. D., 1953. 'Dancing Masks from Somaliland' in *Man*, LIII, pp. 49–51.

Cory, H., 1944. F'igurines used in the initiation ceremonies of the Nguu of Tanganyika' in *Africa*. XIV, pp. 459–64.

Cory, H., 1947, 1948. 'Jando' in *Journal of the Royal Anthropological Institute*, LXXVII, pp. 159–68; LXXVIII, pp. 81–94.

Cory, H., 1956. *African Figurines: Their Ceremonial Use in Puberty Rites in Tanganyika*. London.

Cummins, S. L., 1904. 'Sub-Tribes of the Bahr-el-Ghazal Dinkas' in *Journal of the Royal Anthropological Institute*, XXXIV, pp. 149–166.

Elisofon, E. and Fagg, W., 1958. *The Sculpture of Africa*. London.

Elkan, W., 1958. 'The East African Trade in Woodcarvings' in *Africa*, XXVIII, pp. 314–23

Fagg, W., 1964. *Afrika: 100 Stämme —100 Meisterwerke*. Exhibition Catalogue, Berlin. Also published as: *Afrique: 100 tribus —100 chefs-d'oeuvre*. Exhibition Catalogue, Paris, 1964 and, in expanded form, as *Tribes and Forms in African Art*. London, 1965.

Frobenius, L., 1898. 'Die Masken und Geheimbünde Afrikas' in *Abhandlungen der Kaiserlichen Leopoldinisch-Carolinischen Deutschen Akademie der Naturforscher*, LXXIV. Halle.

Frobenius, L., 1923. *Das unbekannte Afrika*. Munich.

Frobenius, L., 1931. *Erythräa*. Berlin.

Germann, P., 1911. 'Zauberglaube und Mannbarkeitsfeiers bei den Wapare, Deutsch-Ost-Afrika' in *Yearbook of the City Ethnological Museum, Leipzig*, V.

Germann, P., 1958. 'Negerplastiken aus dem Museum für Völkerkunde zu Leipzig' in *Beiträge zur afrikanischen Kunst*. Berlin.

Gutmann, B., 1914. *Volksbuch der Dschagga*. Leipzig.

Haberland, E., 1963a. *Galla Süd-Äthiopiens*. Frankfurt.

Haberland, E., 1963b. 'Grabsteine der Arussi und ihre Beziehung zu megalithischen Denkmälern und Totenmalen anderer äthiopischer Völker' in *Acta ethnographica* XII, pp. 99–138. Budapest.

Hall, R. N., 1905. *Great Zimbabwe*. London.

*Het Masker*. Koninglijk museum voor Schone Kunsten. Exhibition catalogue, Antwerp, 1956.

Himmelheber, H., 1960. *Negerkunst und Negerkünstler*. Braunschweig.

Hofmayr,W., 1925. *Die Schilluk*. Mödling.

Hollis, A. C., 1909. 'A Note on the Graves of Wa-Nyika' in *Man*, IX, p. 145.

Holub, E., 1881. *Sieben Jahre in Südafrika*. Vienna. Also translated: *Seven Years in Southern Africa*. London, 1881.

Jensen, A. E., 1936. *Im Lande des Gada*. Stuttgart.

Junker,W., 1890–92. *Travels in Africa*. London.

Junod, H. A., 1913. *The Life of a South African Tribe (Thonga)*. London.

Karasek, A., Eichhorn. A., 1911, 1913, 1918–1922, 1923–1924. 'Beiträge zur Kenntnis der Waschambaa' in *Baessler-Archiv*, I, pp. 155–222; III, pp. 69–131; VII, pp. 56–98; VIII, pp. 1–53.

Kjersmeier, C., 1938. *Centres de style de la sculpture nègre africaine*. IV. Paris-Copenhagen.

Kollman, P., 1898. *Der Nordwesten unserer ostafrikanischen Kolonie*. Berlin.

Kroll, H., 1933. 'Plastische Menschendarstellungen von der Insel Ukerewe im Victoria-See' in *Ethnol. Anzeiger* I, pp. 142–4. (2nd enlarged edition).

Leuzinger, E., 1962. *Africa: The Art of the Negro Peoples*. London.

Lindblom, K. G., 1920. *The Akamba*. Uppsala.

Luschan, F. von, 1900. 'Afrikanische Lehnstühle' in *Globus*, LXXVII.

Metcalfe, M., 1932. 'Notes on a Nyasaland Dance Mask' in *South African Journal of Science*, XXIX, pp. 687–9.

Meyer, H., 1916. *Die Barundi*. Leipzig.

Mounteney-Jephson, A. G., 1890. *On Emin Pasha and the Rebellion at the Equator*. London.

Murdock, G. P., 1959. *Africa: Its Peoples and their Culture and History*. New York.

Paulme, D., 1953. 'Carved Figures from the White Nile in the Musée de l'Homme' in *Man*, LIII, pp. 113–4.

Rangley,W. H. J., 1949, 1950. '"Nyau" in Kotakota District' in *Nyasaland Journal*, II, III.

Rockling, W., 1942. 'Handwerk und Kunst der Wazaramo' in *Koloniale Rundschau*, XXXIII, pp. 31–7.

Rehse, H., 1910. *Kiziba*. Stuttgart.

Richards, A. I. and Schofield, J. F., 1945. 'Pottery Images or *mbusa* used at the *cisungu* ceremony of the Bemba people of Rhodesia' in *South African Journal of Science*, XLI.

Richards, A. I., 1956. Foreword to H. Cory. *African Figurines*.

Routledge,W. S., 1906. 'An Akikuyu Image' in *Man*, VI, pp. 1–3.

Routledge,W. S., 1910. *With a Prehistoric People: The Akikuyu of British East Africa*. London.

Schweinfurth, G., 1872. 'Völkerskizzen aus dem Gebiete Bahr-el-Ghasal' in *Globus*, XXII, pp. 74–7, 88–90, 225–8.

Schweinfurth, G., 1874. *Im Herzen von Afrika*. Leipzig. Also translated: *The Heart of Africa*.

Schweinfurth, G., 1875. *Artes Africanae*. Leipzig.

Seligman, C. G., 1917. 'A Bongo Funerary Figure' in *Man*, XVII, pp. 97–8.

Seligman, C. G., 1925 'Some little-known tribes of the Southern Sudan' in *Journal of the Royal Anthropological Institute*, LV, pp. 15–36.

Seligman, C. G. and B. Z., 1928. 'The Bari' in *Journal of the Royal Anthropological Institute*, LVIII, pp. 409–79.

Seligman, C. G. and B. Z., 1932. *Pagan Tribes of the Nilotic Sudan*. London.

Stannus, H. S., 1910. 'Notes on some Tribes of British Central Africa' in *Journal of the Royal Anthropological Institute*, XL, pp. 285–335.

Stannus, H. S. and Davey, J. B., 1913. 'The Initiation Ceremony for Boys among the Yao of Nyasaland' in *Journal of the Royal Anthropological Institute*, XLIII, pp. 119–23.

Stannus, H. S., 1922. 'The Wayao of Nyasaland' in *Harvard African Studies*, III.

Stuhlmann, F., 1910. 'Handwerk und Industrie in Ostafrika' in *Abhandlungen des Hamburgischen Kolonialinstitut*, I. Hamburg.

Sydow, E. von, 1954. *Afrikanische Plastik*. Edited by G. Kutscher. Berlin.

Tracey, A., 1960. 'Kamba Carvers' in *African Music*, II.

Trevor, T. G., 1930. 'Some Observations on the Relics of the Pre-European Culture in Rhodesia and South Africa' in *Journal of the Royal Anthropological Institute*, LX, pp. 389–400.

Trowell, K. M., 1947. 'Modern African Art in East Africa' in *Man*, XLVII, 1–7.

Vajda, L., 1953. 'Zum religionsethnologischen Hintergrund des "nungu" im Kilimandscharogebiet' in *Acta ethnographica*, III, pp. 185–232. Budapest.

Vajda, L., 1955. 'Human and Animal Plastic Figures from the Kilimanjaro Region' in *Néprajzi értesítö*, XXXVII, pp. 181–90. Budapest.

Walk, L., 1928. Initiationszeremonien und Pubertätsriten der südafrikanischen Stämme' in *Anthropos*, XXIII, pp. 861–966.

Werner, A., 1915. 'The Bantu Coast Tribes of the East African Protectorate' in *Journal of the Royal Anthropological Institute*, XLV, pp. 326–54.

Westermann, D., 1912. *The Shilluk People: Their Language and Folklore*. Berlin.

Weule, K., 1901. Wissenschaftliche Ergebnisse meiner ethnographischen Forschungsreise in den Südosten Deutsch-Ostafrikas. Mitteilungen aus den Deutschen Schutzgebiete. Ergänzungsband I. Berlin.

Weule, K., 1908. *Negerleben in Ostafrika*. Leipzig. Also translated: *Native Life in East Africa*. London, 1909.

Whitehead, G. O., and Thomas, T., 1938. 'Carved Wood Figures from the Nile' in *Compte rendu, IIéme Congrès Internat. des Sciences anthropologiques et ethnologiques*. Copenhagen.

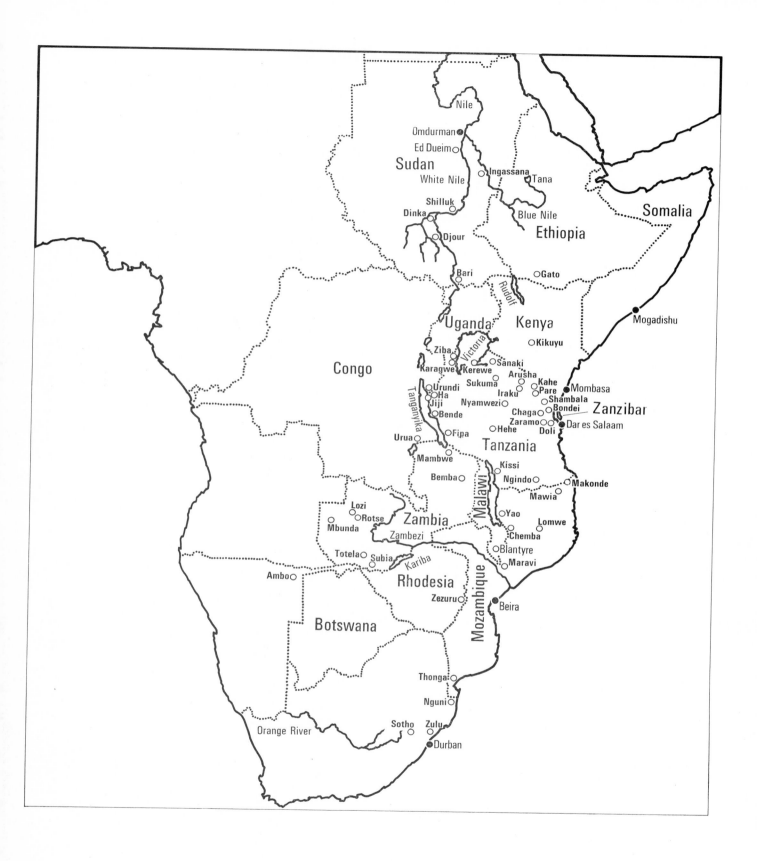

# LIST OF PLATES

| | |
|---|---|
| 83 | Standing female figure. Northern Mozambique. Wood. |
| 84 | Standing female figure. Makonde tribe. Wood. |
| 85 | Woman with child. Makonde tribe. Wood. |
| 86 | Mask. Makonde tribe. Wood. |
| 87 | Mask. Makonde tribe. Wood. |
| 88 | Mask. Makonde tribe. Wood. |
| 89 | Mask. Makonde tribe. Wood. |
| 90 | Mask. Makonde tribe. Wood. |
| 91 | Body mask. Makonde tribe. Wood. |
| 92 | Masks. Makonde tribe. Wood. |
| 93 | Mask. Makonde tribe. Wood. |
| 94 | Mask. Makonde tribe. Wood. |
| 95 | Mask. Makonde tribe. Wood. |
| 96 | Mask. Makonde tribe. Wood. |
| 97 | Mask. Makonde tribe. Wood. |
| 98abc | Mask. Makonde tribe. Wood. |
| 99 | Mask. Makonde tribe. Wood. |
| 100 | Mask. Makonde tribe. Wood. |
| 101 | Mask. Makonde tribe. Wood. |
| 102 | Mask. Yao tribe. Wood. |
| 103 | Toy bull. Makonde tribe. Clay. |
| 104 | Mask. Makonde tribe. Wood. |
| 105 | Staff. Makonde tribe. Wood. |
| 106 | Kneeling female figure. Mawia tribe. Wood. |
| 107 | Standing female figure. Bemba tribe. Wood. |
| 108 | Mask. Eastern Zambia. Composite. |
| 109 | Mask. Mambwe tribe. Wood. |
| 110 | Standing figure. Blantyre region of Malawi. Wood. |
| 111 | Standing female figure. Blantyre region of Malawi. Wood. |
| 112ab | Standing woman with child. Blantyre region of Malawi. Wood. |
| 113 | Standing female figure. Lomwe tribe. Wood. |
| 114abc | Standing female figure. Lomwe tribe. Wood. |
| 115ab | Standing female figure. Maravi tribes. Wood. |
| 116 | Mask. Chemba tribe. Wood. |
| 117 | Food dish. Zambia. Wood. |
| 118 | Food dish. Lozi tribe. Wood. |
| 119 | Food dish. Lozi tribe. Wood. |
| 120 | Stool. Lozi tribe. Wood. |
| 121 | Food dish. Lozi tribe. Wood. |
| 122ab | Kneeling woman with dish. Lozi tribe. Wood. |
| 123ab | Standing female figure. Lozi tribe(?). Horn. |
| 124 | Mask. Mbunda tribe. Wood. |
| 125 | Headrest. Totela tribe. Wood. |
| 126 | Pottery vessel. Zezuru tribes. Pottery. |
| 127 | Pottery vessel. Zezuru tribes. Pottery. |
| 128 | Pottery vessel. Zezuru tribes. Pottery. |
| 129 | Mask. Zezuru tribes. Wood. |
| 130 | Standing figures. Nguni/Thonga tribes. Wood. |
| 131 | Standing female figure. Nguni/Thonga tribes. Wood. |
| 132 | Standing figures. Thonga/Magwamba tribes. Wood. |
| 133 | Standing figures. Nguni/Thonga tribes. Wood. |
| 134 | Standing figures. Nguni/Thonga tribes. Wood. |
| 135 | Standing female figure. Zulu tribe. Wood. |
| 136ab | Standing male figure. Zulu tribe. Wood. |
| 137 | Standing male figure. Zulu tribe. Wood. |
| 138 | Standing female figure. Zulu tribe. Wood. |
| 139 | Staffs. Zulu tribe. Wood. |
| 140 | Headrests. Nguni/Zulu tribes. Wood. |
| 141 | Doll. Zulu tribe. Composite. |
| 142 | Doll. Zulu tribe. Composite. |
| 143 | Bull. Sotho tribe. Clay. |
| 144 | Animal figure. Sotho tribe. Clay. |
| 145 | Bull. Sotho tribe. Clay. |
| 146 | Bull. Sotho tribe. Clay. |
| 147 | Doll. Sotho tribe. Composite. |
| 148 | Doll. Ambo tribe. Composite. |
| 149 | Doll. Sotho tribe. Composite. |
| 150 | Doll. Ambo tribe. Composite. |
| 151 | Headrest. Ambo tribe. Composite. |
| 152 | Doll. Ambo tribe. Composite. |

# PLATES

2

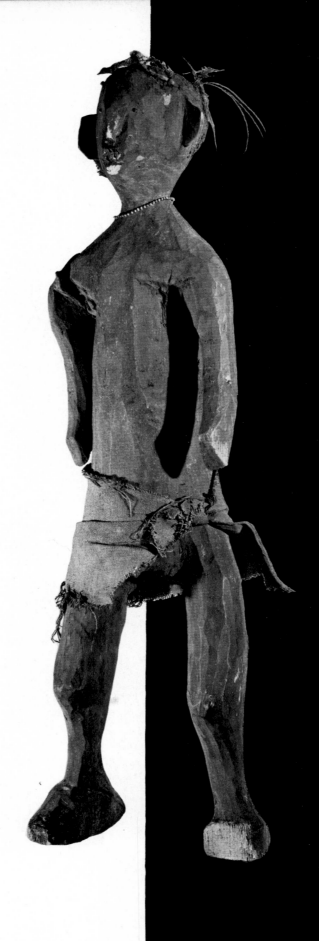

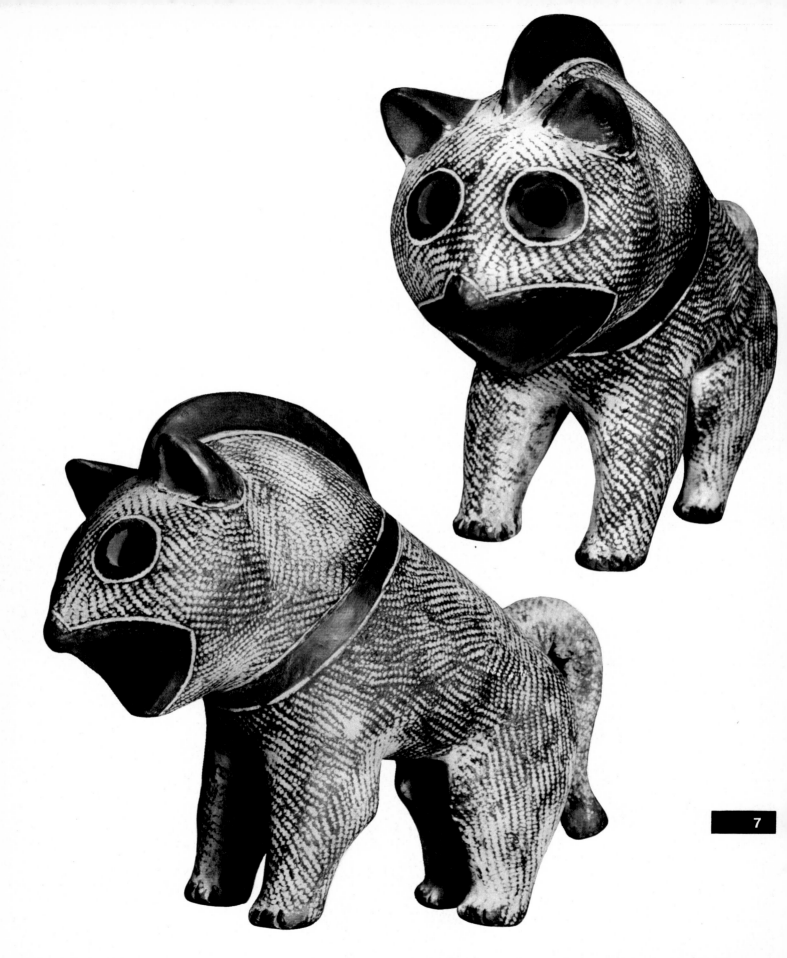

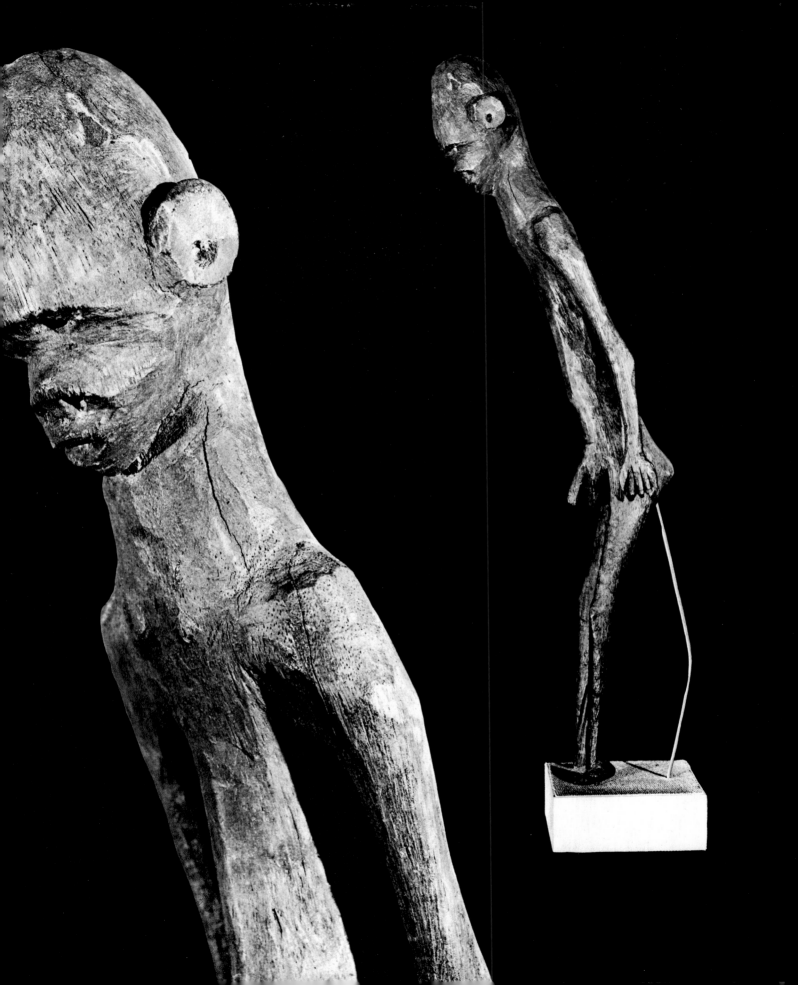

15

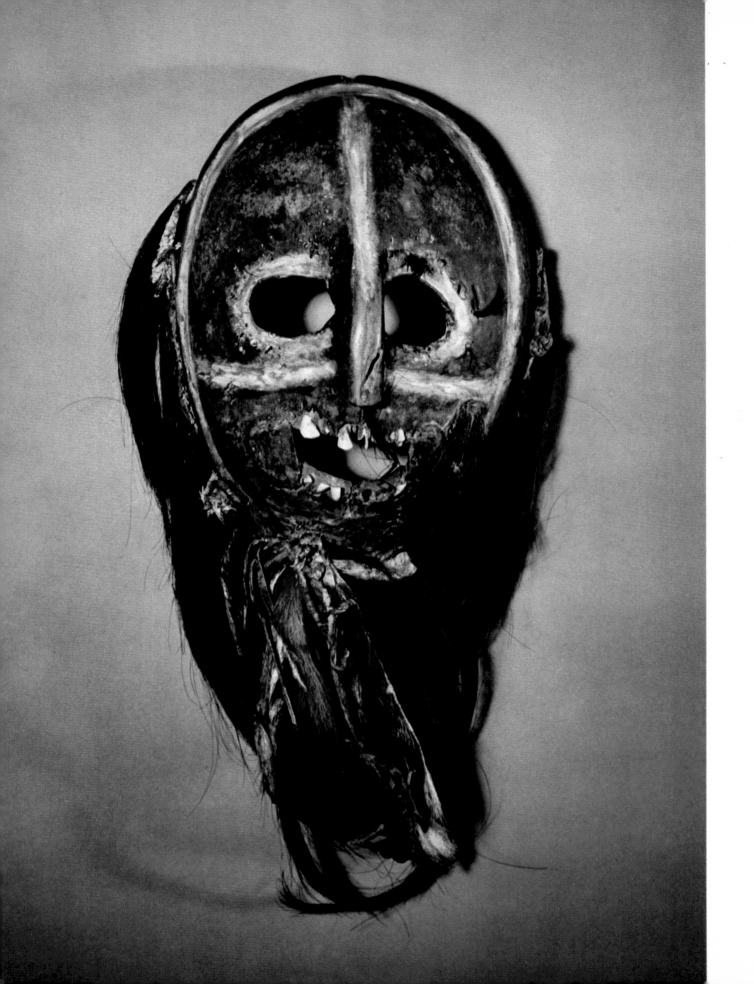

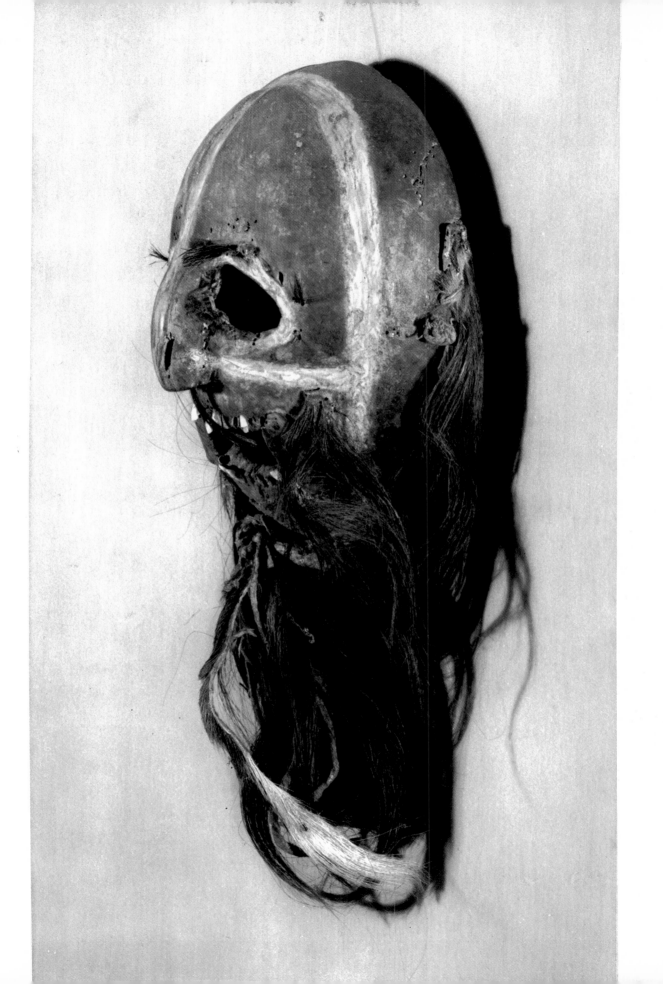

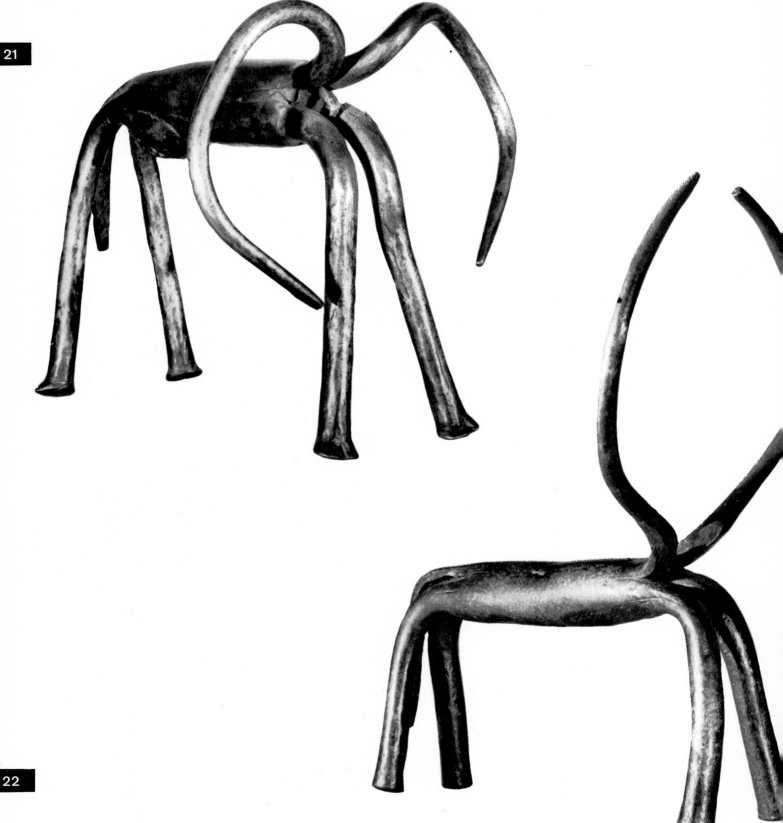

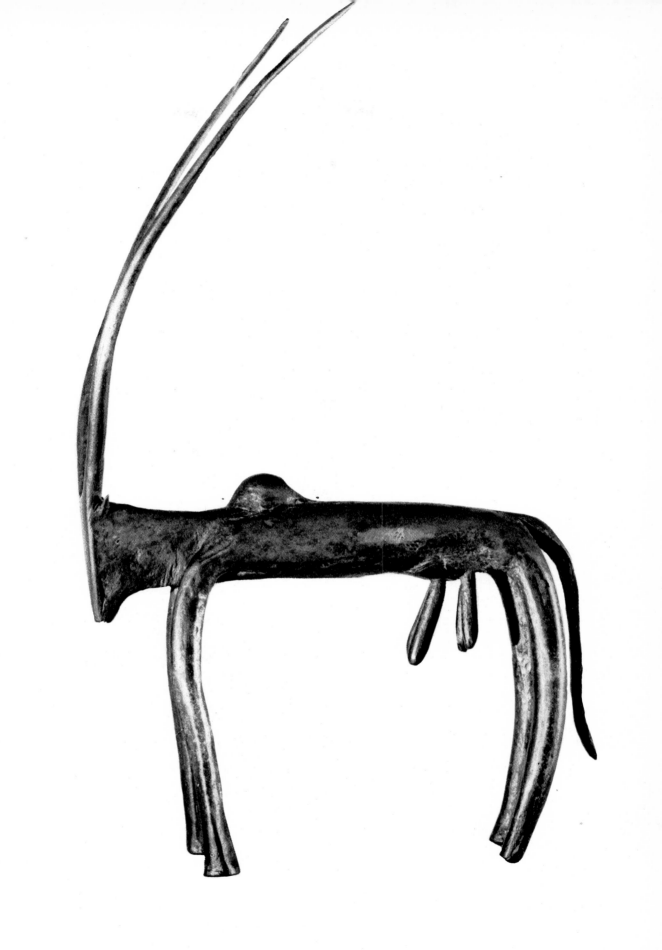

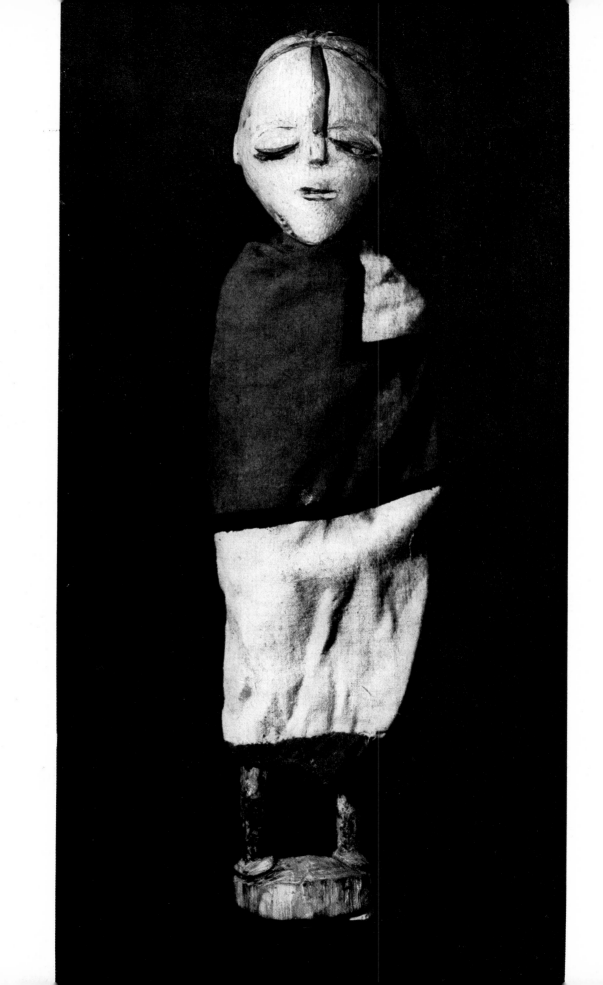

29

30

31

32 33

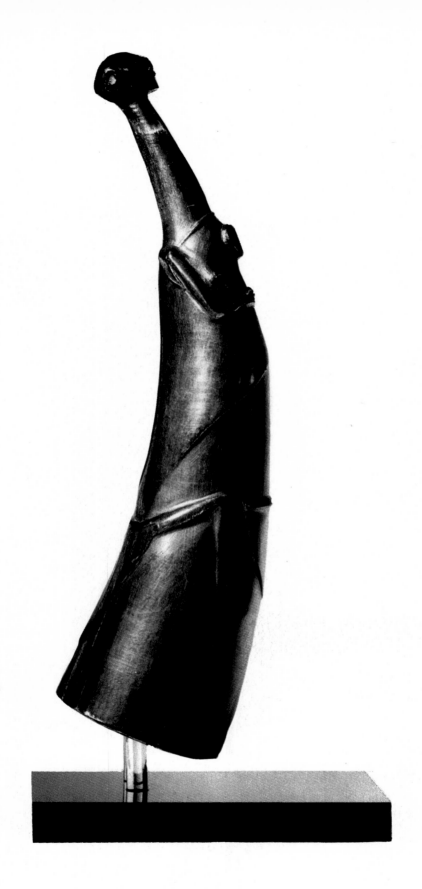

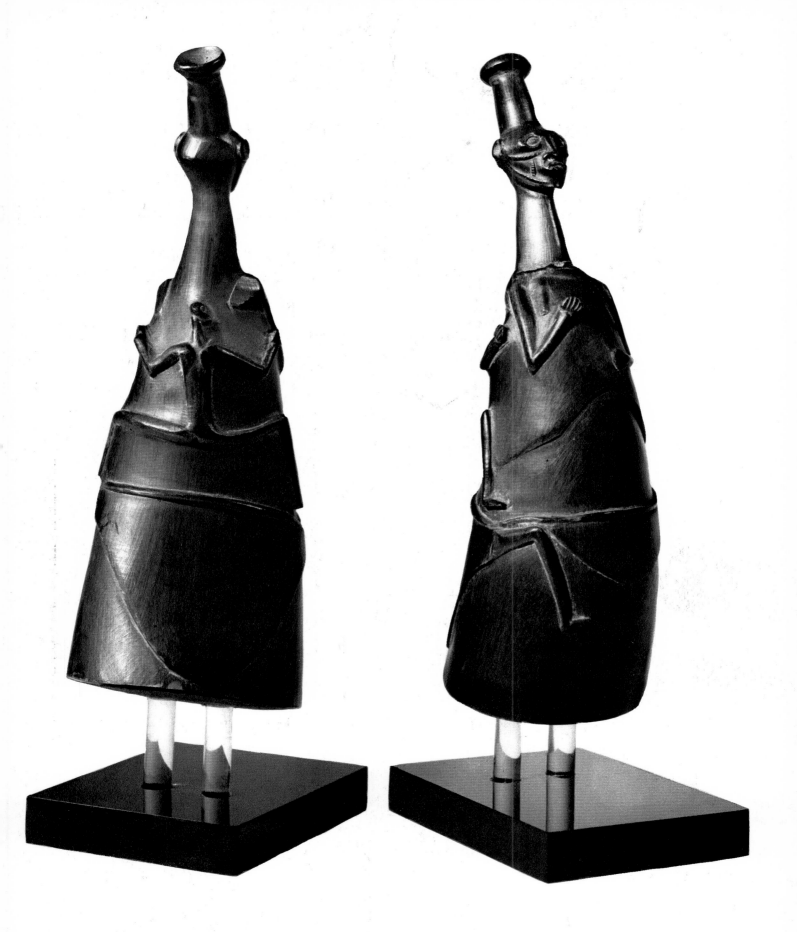

41

42

50

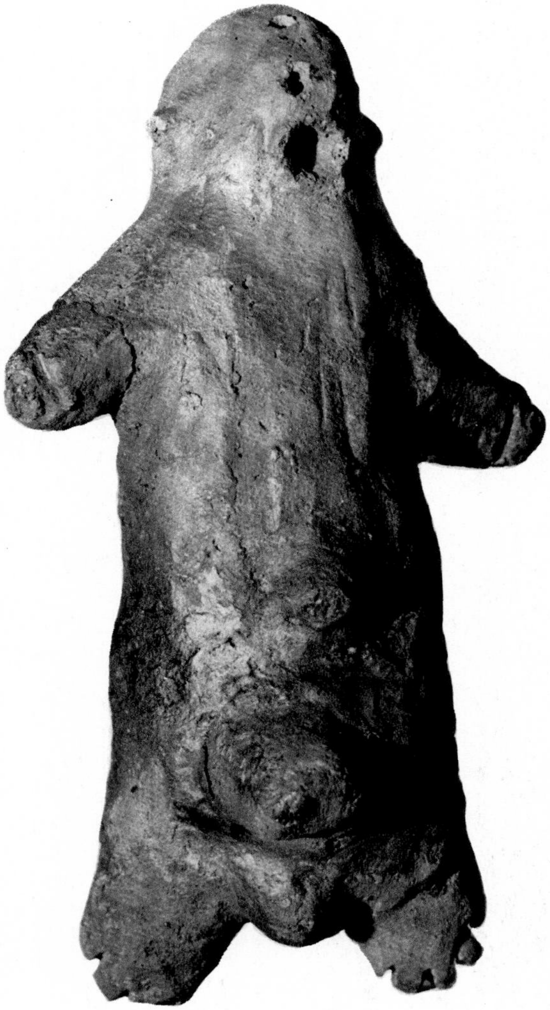

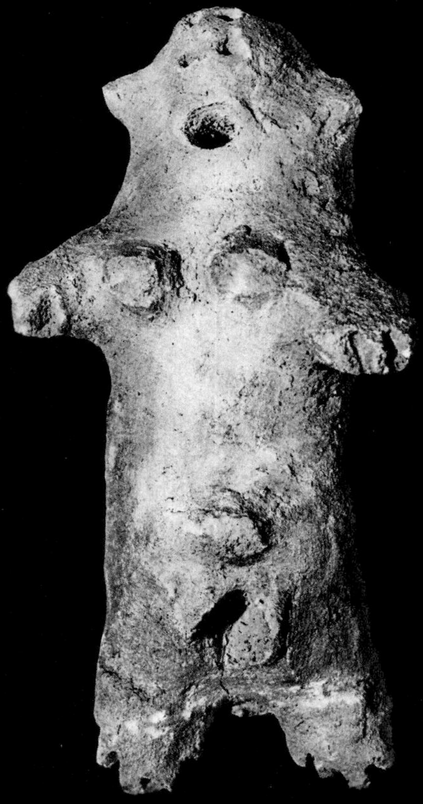

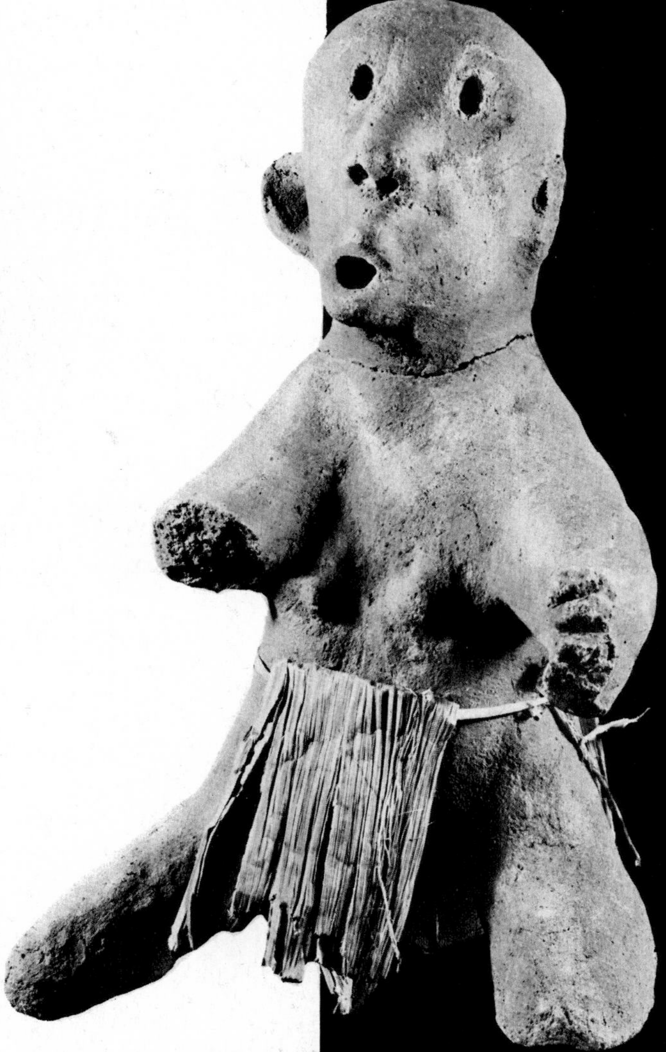

53

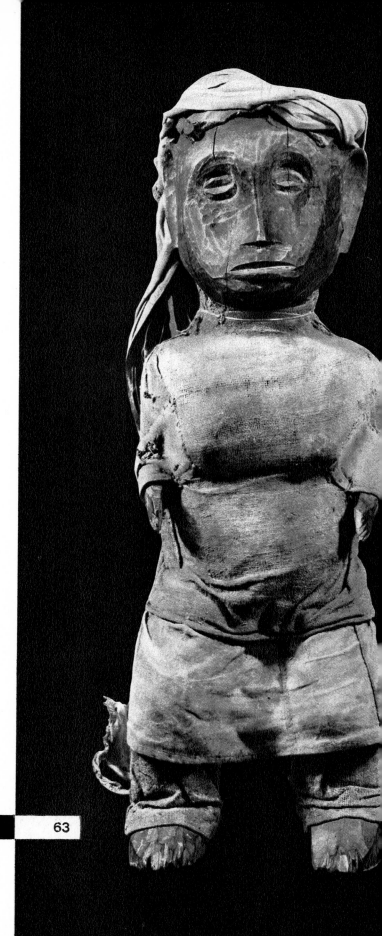

62          63

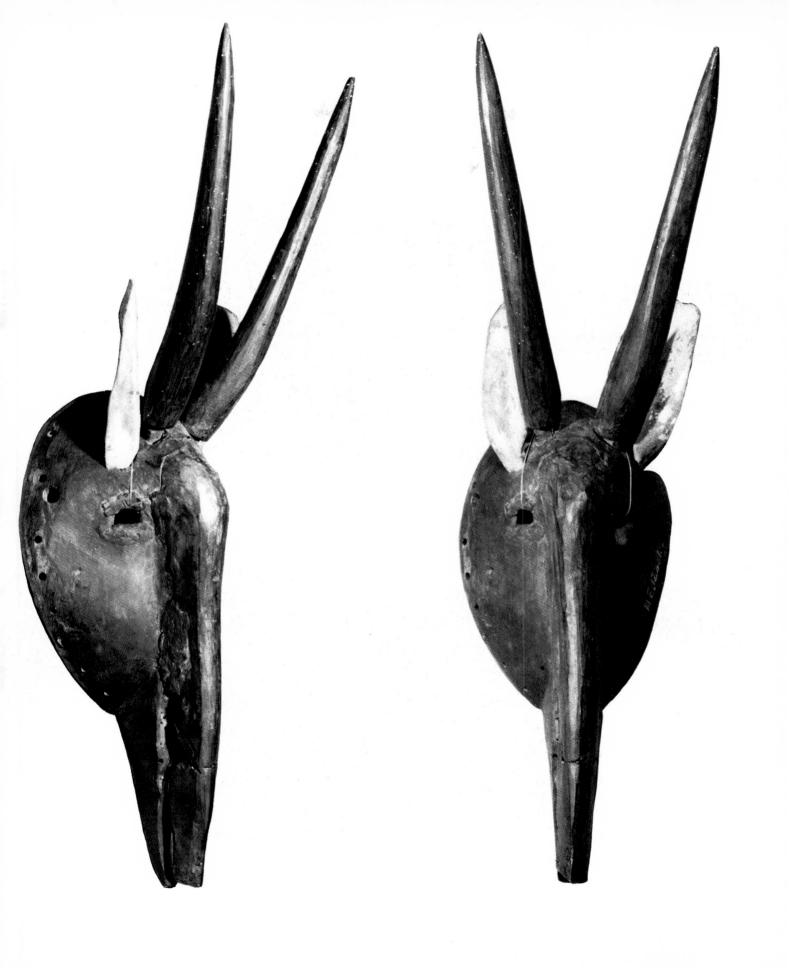

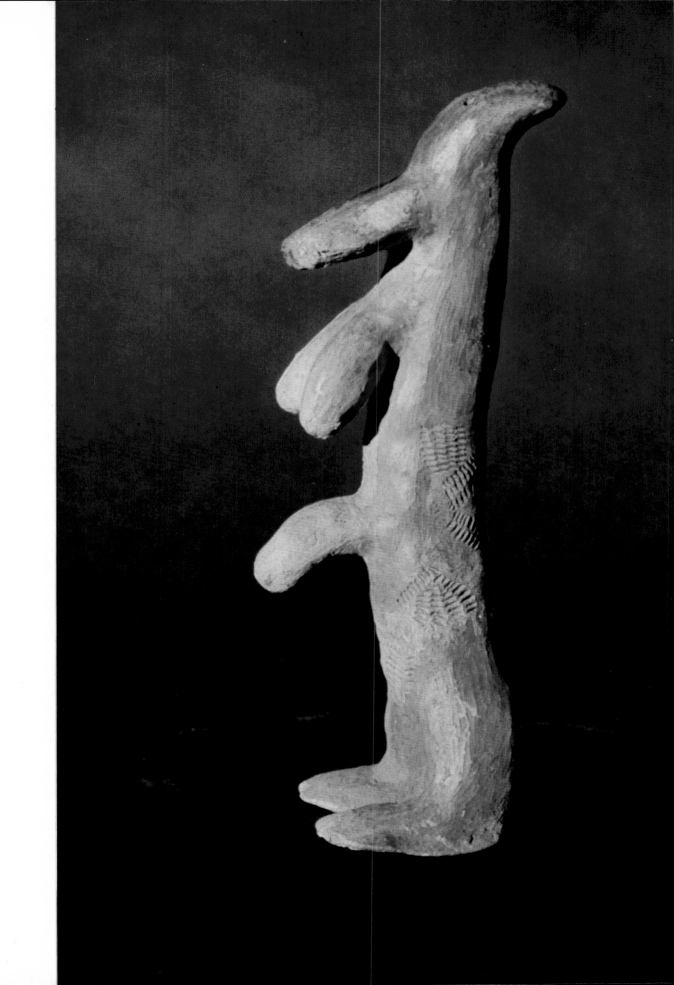

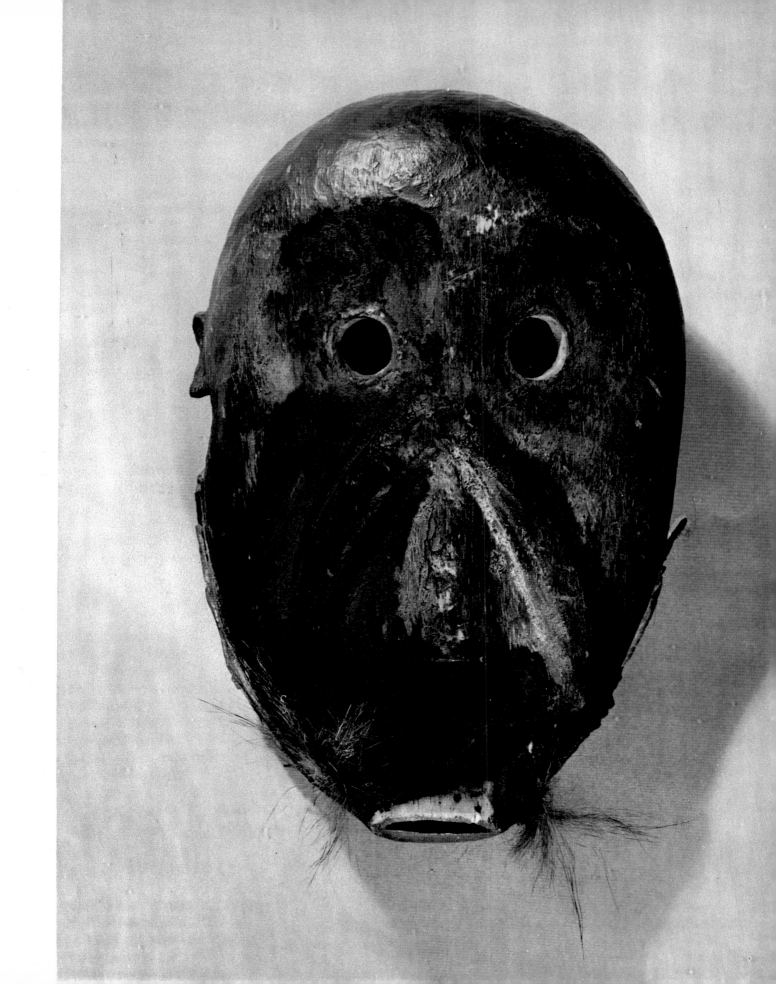

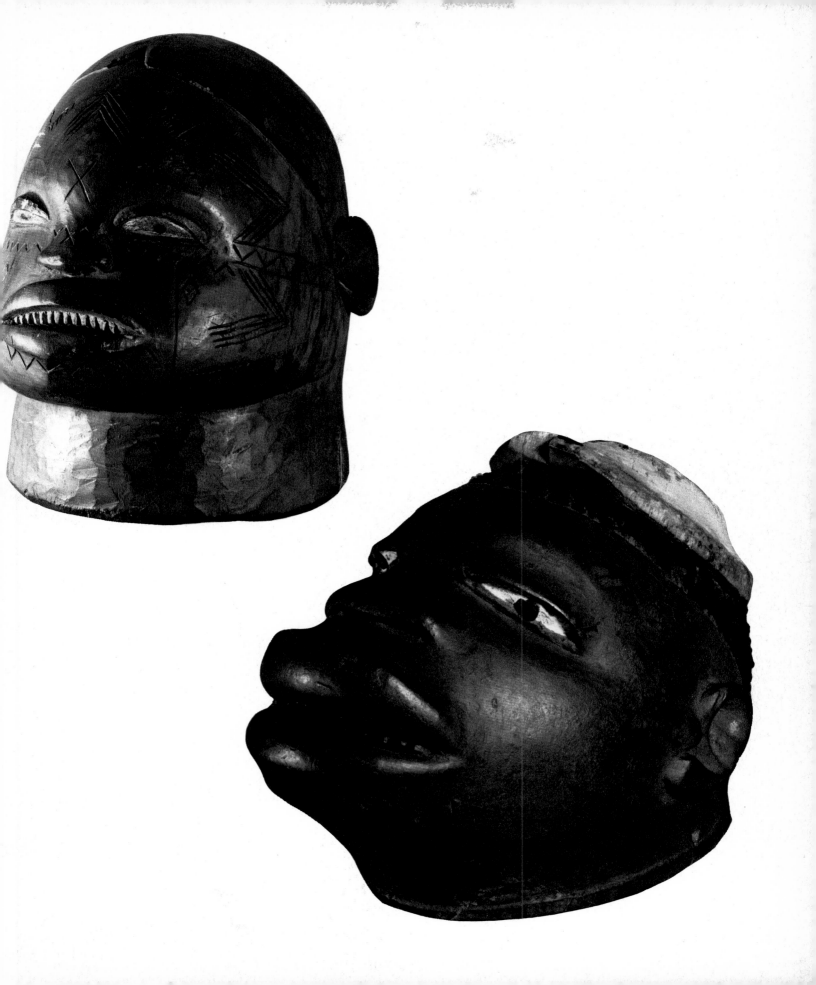

81    82

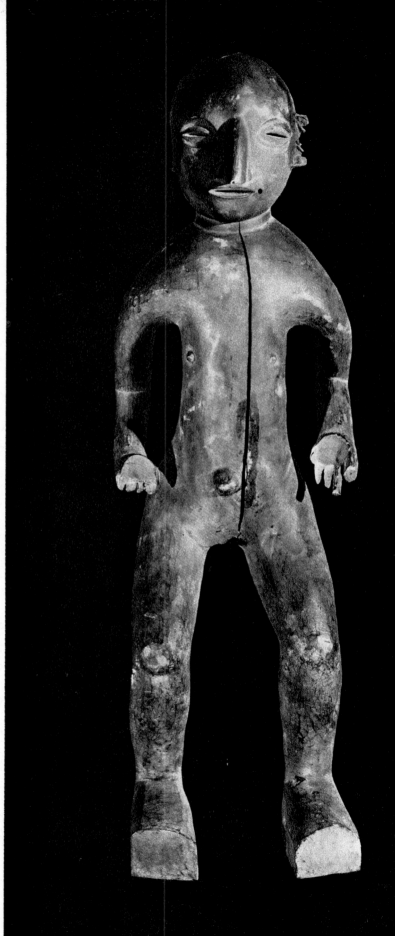

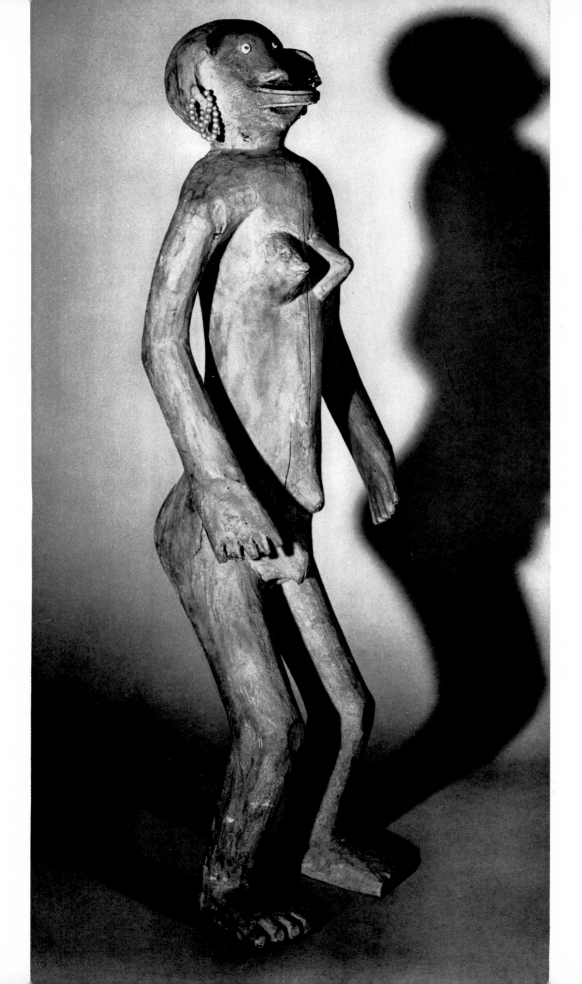

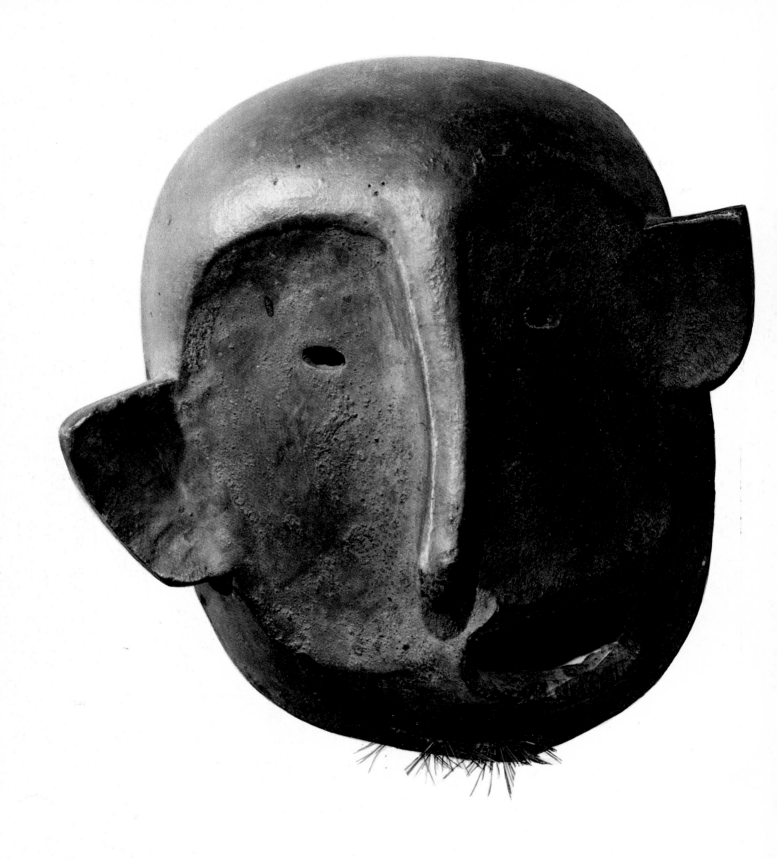

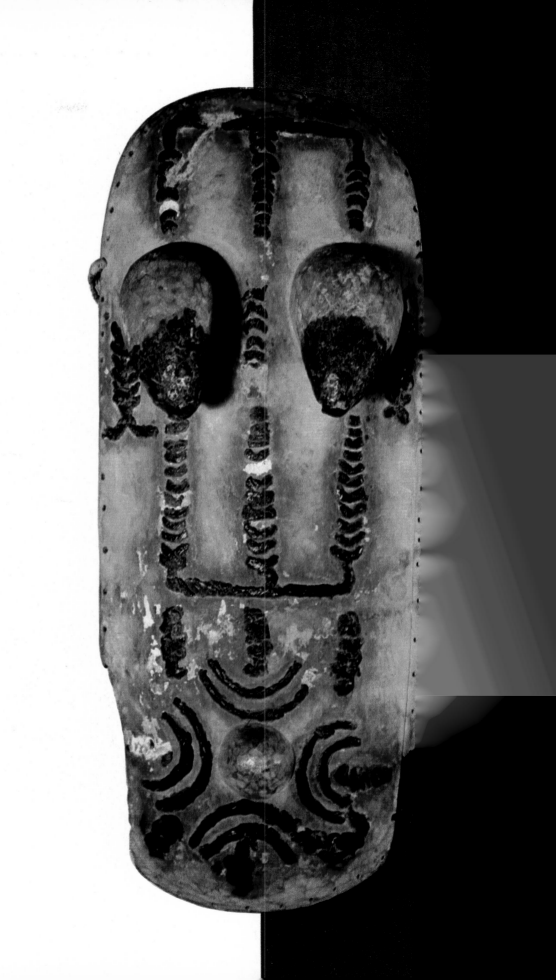

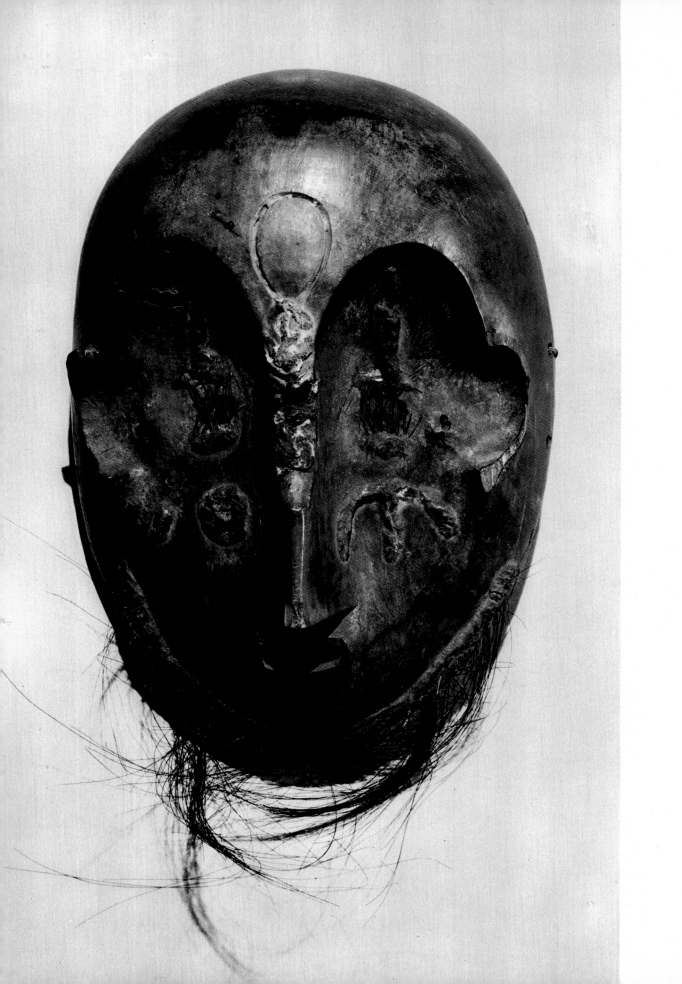

99    100

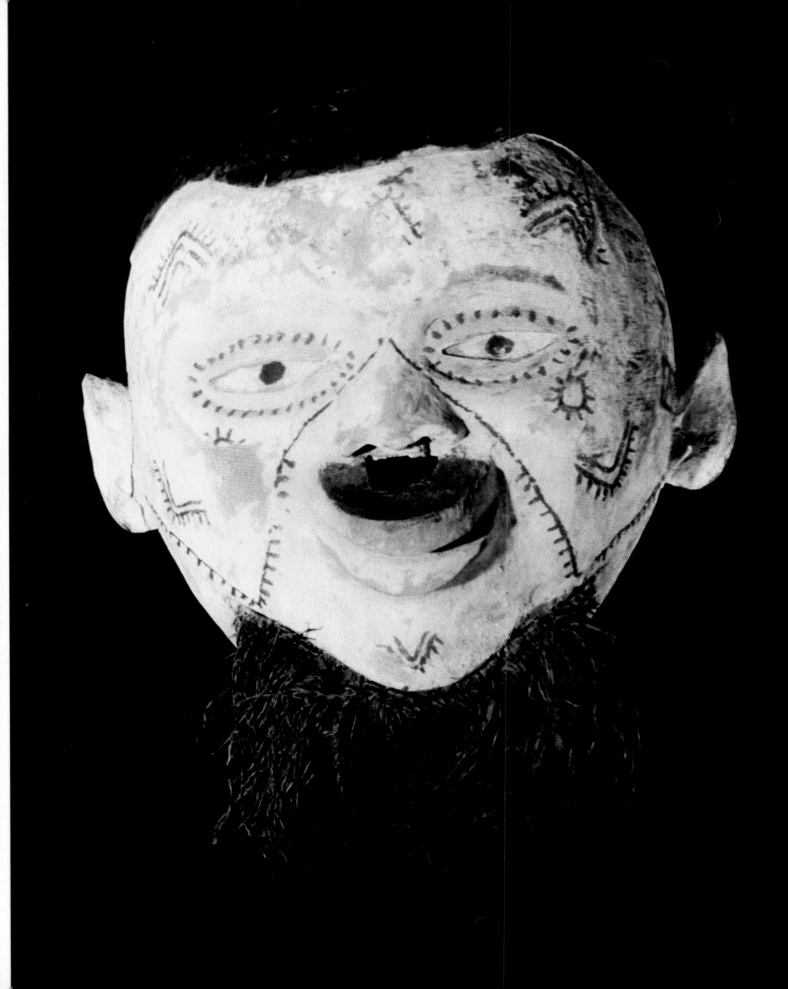

105          106

110 111

113          114

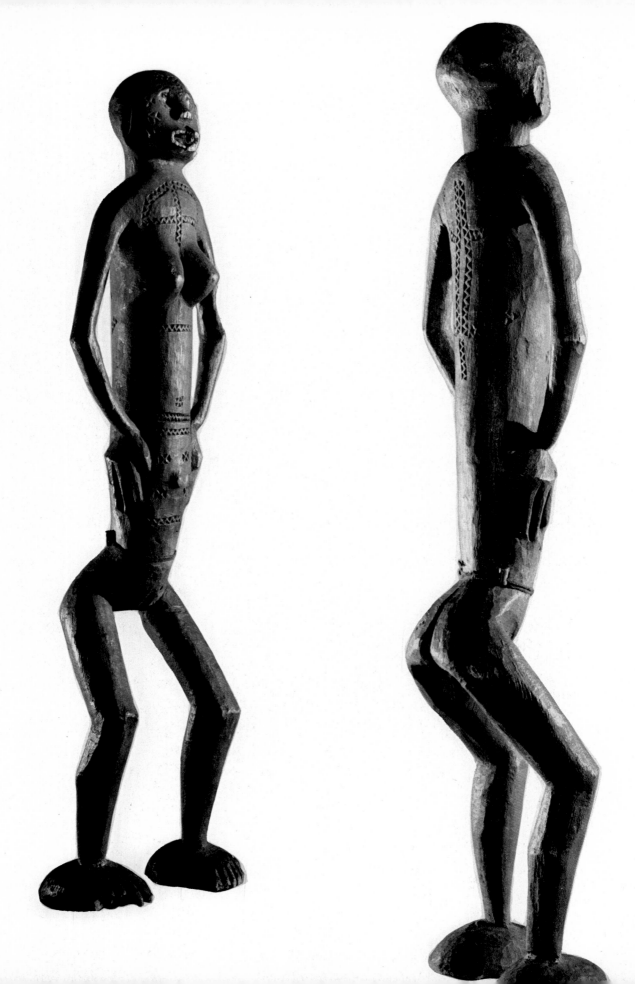

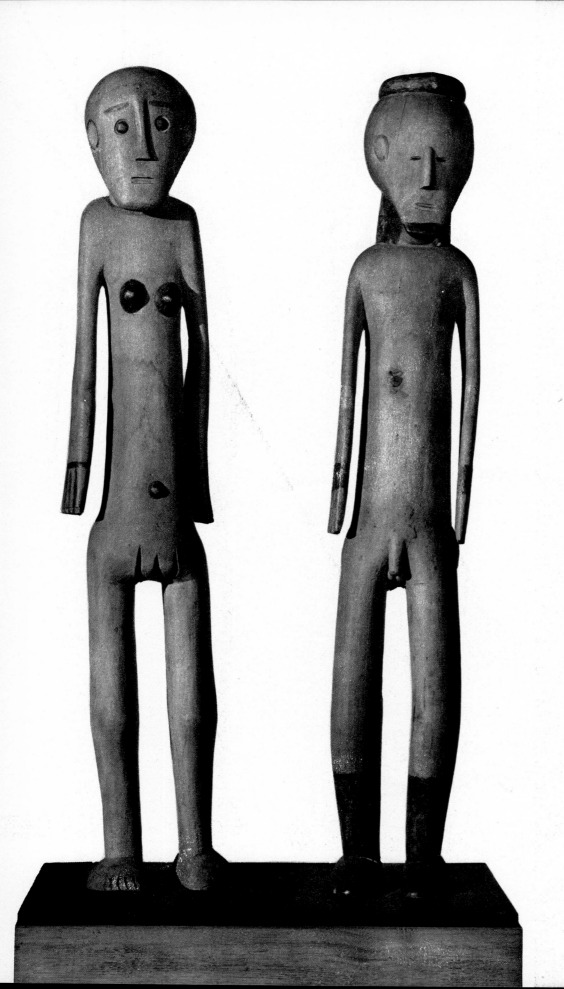

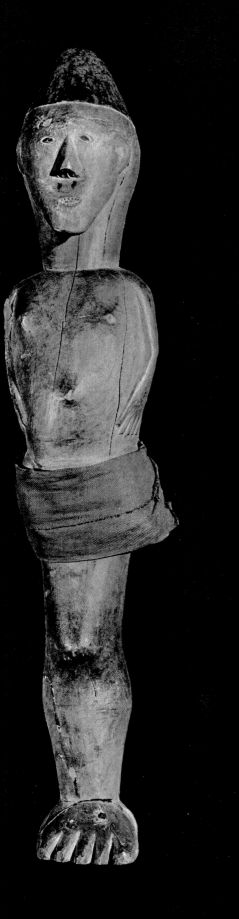

135 136

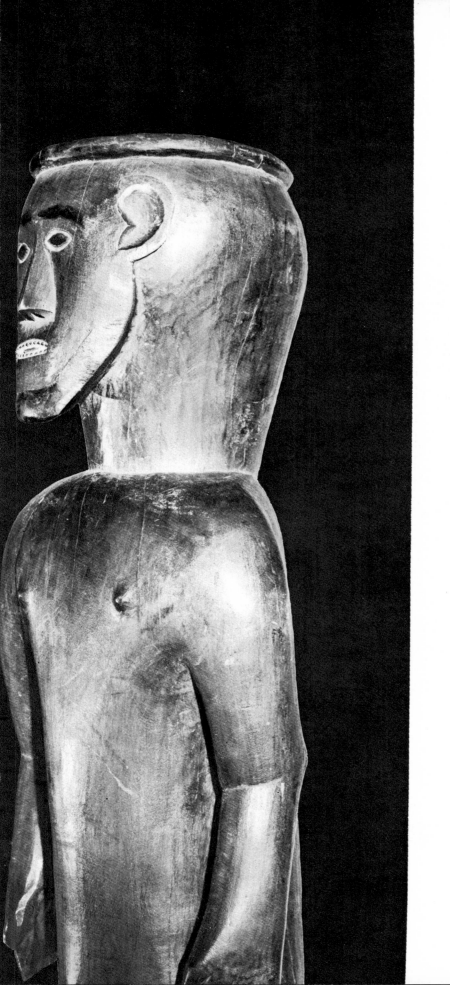

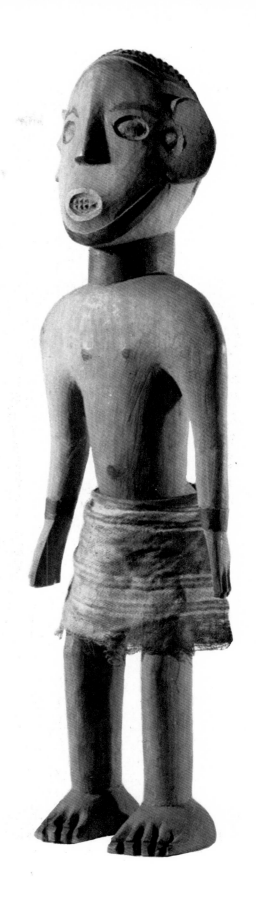

138

139

143

144

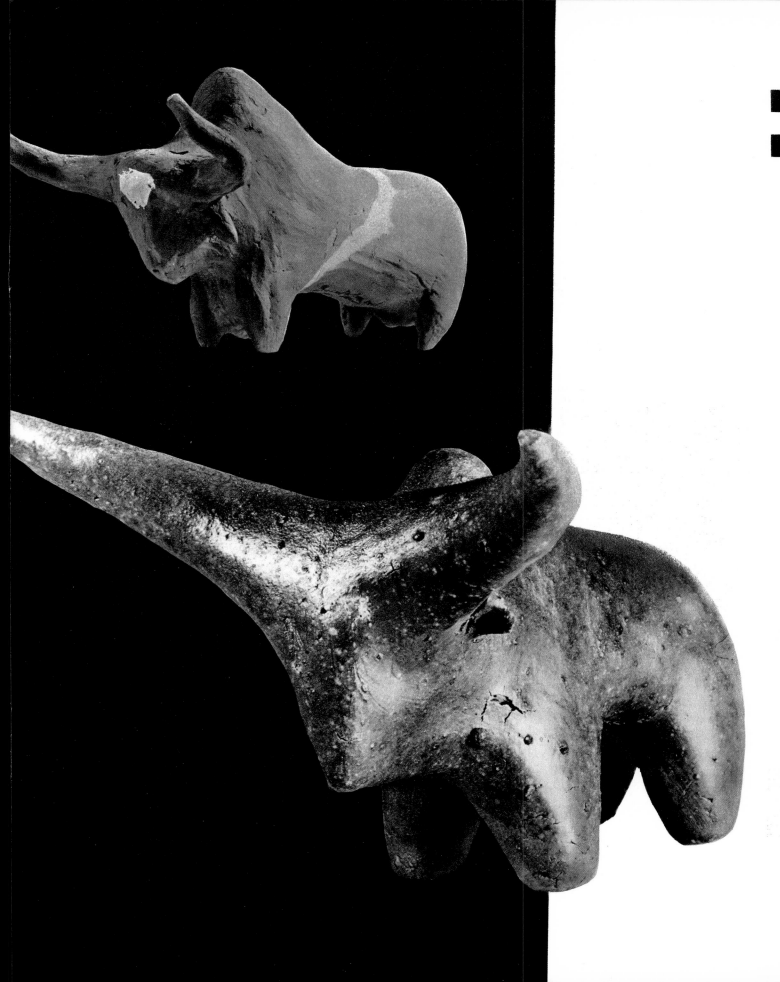

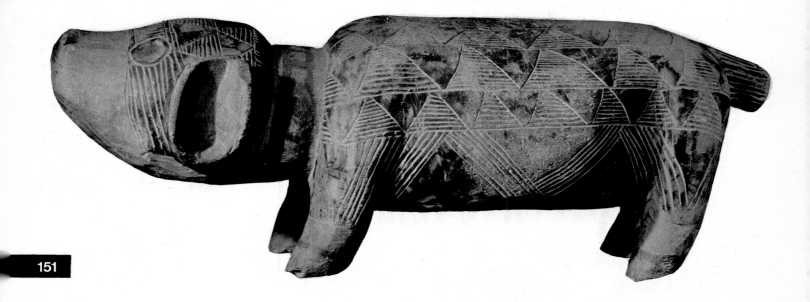